Library Basics Series

Learn Dewey Decimal Classification (Edition 21)

Mary Mortimer

Library Basics, No. 2

The Scarecrow Press, Inc.
Lanham, Maryland, and London
in cooperation with
DocMatrix Pty Ltd, Canberra, Australia
2000

SCARECROW PRESS, INC.

Published in the United States of America
by Scarecrow Press, Inc.
4720 Boston Way, Lanham, Maryland 20706
http://www.scarecrowpress.com

4 Pleydell Gardens, Folkestone
Kent CT20 2DN, England

Design by Andrew Rankine Design Associates pty ltd, Canberra, Australia

British Library and National Library of Australia Cataloguing in Publication Information
Available

Library of Congress Cataloging-in-Publication Data

Mortimer, Mary, 1944-
    Learn Dewey Decimal Classification (Edition 21) / Mary Mortimer.
      p. cm.
    ISBN 0-8108-3694-7 (alk. paper)
    1. Classification, Dewey decimal.   I. Title.
Z696.D7M66 2000
026.4'31—dc21   99-40185
                                    CIP

CONTENTS

PREFACE

This book covers the skills necessary for a classifier using Dewey Decimal Classification in a library or other information agency, whether at a professional or a paraprofessional level. It is equally suitable for use by students studying library science in universities and colleges and others who are studying classification by themselves, either with a specific goal or as part of their continuing professional development. Since most collections are organized according to a library classification scheme, and Dewey Decimal Classification is widely used, especially in public and school libraries, it is important for all library students and most library staff to be familiar with at least the basics.

Throughout the book you will find exercises to practice and test your skills and quizzes to test your understanding. There are answers for self-checking at the back of the book. You may not always agree completely with the answers given, and it is useful to check them with a teacher or experienced classifier. Despite the best endeavors of the editors of DDC to standardize the allocation of numbers, there is often room for more than one interpretation or emphasis.

ACKNOWLEDGMENTS

Thanks to my Australian colleagues and students for their suggestions, corrections, and encouragement.

Chapter 1
INTRODUCTION TO CLASSIFICATION

Introduction
A classification scheme organizes subjects systematically and shows their relationships.

EXERCISE 1.1
Write down some examples of classification other than library classification:

Library Classification
The basic principle of library classification is to group the items on the shelves according to their subject content, or sometimes literary or bibliographic form.

Works which are used together should be shelved together.

Literary warrant—i.e., the volume of works which have been written, or are likely to be written, on any topic—should be a primary factor in the formulation of a classification scheme.

The Library of Congress Classification scheme is heavily based on this idea, since it was developed using the material actually held in the Library of Congress when the scheme was being developed.

Purposes of Library Classification
Library classification schemes serve to
- bring related items together in a helpful sequence
- provide formal orderly access to the shelves either through a direct search of the shelves (browsing) or via the catalog
- enable easy reshelving of library materials
- provide an order for the classified catalog.

Types of Classification

Enumerative classification attempts to spell out (enumerate) all the single and composite subject concepts required:

> e.g., Library of Congress Classification and, to a lesser extent, Dewey Decimal Classification (DDC)

Synthetic classification, also called faceted classification, lists numbers for single concepts and allows the classifier to construct (synthesize) numbers for composite subjects:

> e.g., Colon Classification, Universal Decimal Classification, some features of DDC.

Hierarchical classification is based on the division of subjects from the most general to the most specific:

> e.g., Dewey Decimal Classification, Library of Congress Classification (to a much lesser extent).

Features of a Classification Scheme

Library classification schemes generally have the following features:

- schedules
- notation
- index
- number building.

Schedules

The schedules are the printed, enumerated classes, divisions, etc., of the scheme, arranged in number order. Schedules range from fairly sparse to extremely detailed. In general, the more enumerative the scheme, the more detailed the schedules; the more synthetic, the slimmer the schedules.

The Library of Congress Classification schedules are much lengthier than the Dewey Decimal Classification schedules, since DDC relies more on number building, whereas LCC lists more of its numbers.

In addition, schedules usually have

- a generalities class
- form classes
- form divisions.

The generalities class is used for very general topics, and comprehensive combinations of topics, e.g., current affairs, general encyclopedias.

Form classes are used for literature. That is, items are grouped not according to subject but according to the literary form—poetry, drama, prose, etc.—in which they are written. These classes also include literary criticism.

Form divisions are used for works on any subject which are presented in a particular bibliographic form, e.g., dictionary, periodical.

Notation

The notation of a classification scheme is the series of symbols which stand for the classes, subclasses, divisions, and subdivisions of classes.

Notation is used to

- indicate a subject
- show its relationship to a class
- provide a sequential order for arrangement.

Pure notation is the use of only one type of symbol, such as numbers—e.g., Dewey Decimal Classification 342.569.

Mixed notation is the use of more than one type of symbol, such as numbers and letters—e.g., Library of Congress Classification TK51011.H37 1994.

Good notation should

- convey order clearly and automatically
- be as brief and simple as possible
- be easy to say, write, and remember
- be flexible, allowing insertion at any point without dislocating the sequence
- facilitate the use of mnemonics (memory aids)

Index

The index is the alphabetical list of the terms used in the schedules, together with the corresponding notation. It provides access to the schedules. It should include, as far as possible, all synonyms for the term and a breakdown of parts of the subject.

There are two types of index:

- specific—with only one entry for each topic mentioned in the schedules
- relative—enumerating all topics and synonyms and showing the relation of each topic to all the disciplines in which it is found.

Number Building

This is the ability of the scheme to allow the construction of notation to include items not specifically mentioned in the schedules.

Criteria of a Successful Classification Scheme

- It should create an order convenient to the user—the main purpose of classification.
- It should be as complete as possible, covering the whole field of knowledge.
- It should proceed from the general to the specific.
- It should be evenly apportioned, so that subjects of equal importance have roughly equivalent space in the schedules.
- It should have - generalities and form classes,
  - form and geographical divisions,
  - effective notation, and
  - an alphabetical index.
- It should be able to accommodate new notation as knowledge expands—e.g., new classifications such as computers, environmental issues.

- The terms must be clear and easy to understand, accompanied where necessary by full definitions, the scope of headings, and notes to guide the classifier.
- It should be printed in a form which is easy to handle and consult and enables the user to grasp the structure.
- It must be revised frequently to keep up with new knowledge, new interpretations, and new emphases in the presentation of knowledge.

EXERCISE 1.2

On a large sheet of paper, create a plan of a zoo to house the following animals. Your plan must show some logical system for grouping the animals, although how you do this is up to you.

aardvark	alligator	anaconda	antelope	bison	black swan
brown bear	camel	Cape hunting dog	cheetah	cobra	cockatoo
condor	crocodile	deer	dingo	Indian elephant	emu
frilled-neck lizard	giraffe	goanna	gorilla	hippopotamus	
ibis	jaguar	kangaroo	koala	Komodo dragon	kookaburra
leopard	lion	mongoose	monkey	mountain goat	
orangutan	ostrich	panther	pelican	platypus	polar bear
tiger	tortoise	water buffalo	white rhinoceros	wolf	zebra

The Needs of the User

A library's classification policy needs to take account of its users and their needs. For example, many public library users regard biographies as a "good read", and are less concerned with the specialization of a famous person than with the interesting life he or she has led. So public libraries are likely to house their biographies together, using the number for general biography, or even the simple location symbol "B". A medical library, on the other hand, is more likely to classify the biographies of medical researchers with the diseases or treatments they have spent much of their lives studying.

How closely a work is classified should also take a library's users into account. A library which has only a few books about bridges does not need to differentiate between concrete bridges, wooden bridges, metal bridges, and so on. However an engineering library with a large collection of works about bridges may decide to classify them very specifically to assist users to find exactly what they want.

A library may supply its catalogers with a list of particular numbers (e.g., for literature) or a statement of general policy (e.g., no more than 8 digits after the decimal point). If the policy is to shorten numbers, the classifier must take care that the number is not reduced arbitrarily, but is still a meaningful number within the classification scheme.

When libraries use another source as the basis for their records (copy cataloging), they need to ensure that the classification number is consistent with their own cataloging and classification policies. This requires familiarity with the policies as well as the classification scheme.

Individual catalogers also make judgments about classification in relation to the library's users, in the same way as other aspects of cataloging take them into account.

Different Sequences

A library usually has several sequences of works in its collection. These can include fiction, non-fiction books for loan, reference works (not for loan), periodicals, children's books, audiovisual materials (which may be divided into different formats—videos, compact discs), and so on.

Fiction is usually indicated by the location symbol "F" and arranged alphabetically by author's surname. Periodicals are sometimes classified, using the same scheme as the main collection, and sometimes arranged alphabetically by title.

Other parts of the collection are either classified, using the same classification scheme, or arranged alphabetically or by their own number (e.g., ISO standards) within their sequence. When a library acquires material in a new format, a decision is made about whether to integrate the material into an existing sequence or house the material separately. If a new sequence is established, a new location and the basis for organizing the material will also be decided.

REVIEW QUIZ 1.3

Use the following questions to revise your understanding of library classification. You do not need to write down the answers.

1. Give three reasons for classifying a library collection.

2. What is the difference between enumerative and synthetic classification? Give examples.

3. In what order are classification schedules arranged? Why?

4. What is number building? Why is it a desirable feature of a classification scheme?

5. What is hierarchical classification? How does it work?

6. Why should a library consider the nature of its client group when it classifies its material?

Chapter 2
INTRODUCTION TO DEWEY DECIMAL CLASSIFICATION

Introduction

The Dewey Decimal Classification was developed by Melvil Dewey between 1873 and 1876, when the first edition was published anonymously under the title *A Classification and Subject Index for Cataloguing and Arranging the Books and Pamphlets of a Library*. At that time, libraries used "fixed location" to classify books—that is, the books were kept in a fixed physical space in the library and numbered according to their room, tier, and shelf. They therefore had to be reclassified whenever the library grew beyond its shelving capacity. Dewey's invention of relative location—numbering books according to their intellectual content—formed the basis of library classification as we know it today.

The first edition of his scheme was a 44-page pamphlet and was based on Dewey's view of the world of knowledge which is still used today. The scheme was criticized at the time for being too lengthy. It was, however, an immediate success, and in its succeeding editions has become the most widely used classification scheme, being translated into many languages.

The Dewey editorial office has been located in the Decimal Classification Division of the Library of Congress since 1923. The Division allocates over 110,000 numbers annually to works cataloged by the Library of Congress. The editor and three assistant editors responsible for updating DDC work closely with classification specialists, so that they can detect trends in the published literature.

The Decimal Classification Editorial Policy Committee (EPC) is a ten-member international board which advises the editors of DDC on the development of the Classification. EPC represents the interests of all DDC users, and responds to suggestions from many countries and different types of libraries.

DDC is now in its 21st edition, published in 1996. In recent times it has been revised every eight to ten years. There is also an abridged version, now in its 13th edition. Between editions the scheme is kept up-to-date with additions and corrections published in *Dewey Decimal Classification: Additions, Notes and Decisions (DC&)*.

In 1993 a DOS version of the 20th edition, called *Electronic Dewey*, was published on CD-ROM. In addition to the schedules, tables, Relative Index, and Manual, *Electronic Dewey* also contains some linked Library of Congress subject headings and sample bibliographic records. *Dewey for Windows*, a Microsoft Windows®-based version of *Electronic Dewey*, was published at the same time as Edition 21. It contains all the features of *Electronic Dewey*, together with enhancements made possible by the Windows environment. Users can simultaneously display multiple records or different views of the scheme and move data between windows. *Dewey for Windows* can be loaded onto a network, and users can annotate their records to reflect local classification decisions.

The scheme is published by Forest Press. In 1988, Forest Press became a division of OCLC Online Computer Library Center, Inc.

Format of DDC

The 21st edition of DDC is published in four volumes with over 4,000 pages:

Volume 1   Introduction, glossary and Tables 1-7
Volume 2   Schedules 000-599
Volume 3   Schedules 600-999
Volume 4   Relative Index and Manual

General Characteristics of DDC

Hierarchy

DDC is a hierarchical classification, proceeding from the general to the specific in terms of discipline and subject relationships.

The basic arrangement is by discipline, and the same subject may appear in a number of disciplines. The various aspects of a subject are brought together by the Relative Index.

There are ten classes (see the first summary). Each of the classes from 100 to 900 represents a broad discipline or group of disciplines, whereas the 000 class contains general subjects (generalities) which are not necessarily related disciplines, e.g., newspapers, encyclopedias, computers, and library science.

Each class has ten divisions, represented by the second digit of the notation (see the second summary).

Each division has ten sections, represented by the third digit of the notation (see the third summary).

This hierarchical structure is continued and incorporated in the notation, which is lengthened by one digit for each more specific aspect of the subject.

For example,

600	Technology (Applied sciences)
640	Home economics and family living
646	Sewing, clothing, management of personal and family living
646.7	Management of personal and family living Grooming
646.72	Care of hair, face, skin
646.724	Care of hair
646.7248	Wigs

Number Building

Over 23,000 numbers are listed in the schedules. However DDC also uses number building to expand the classification scheme and create even more specific numbers.

Numbers are constructed by taking a number from the schedules and adding to it digits from Tables 1-7, or from another part of the schedules.

Tables 1 to 7 allow the classifier to make numbers more specific in relation to time periods, places, types of persons, language, literary form, and so on. For example, the geographic aspect of almost any subject can be included by adding one or more digits from Table 2 (Geographic Areas, Historical Periods, Persons).

Tables in the schedules enable aspects, or facets, of one subject to be applied to another subject. For example, many aspects of particular animals and animal groups are listed only once in the schedules, but can be added to any of the animals with classification numbers between 592 and 599.

The Relative Index

No one class can cover all the aspects of a subject. For many subjects, different aspects are located in different classes. The Relative Index brings together (relates) the different aspects of a topic and the different classes in which they are to be found. Here are some of the entries for the topic Metals:

Metals	669
applied nutrition	613.285
architectural construction	721.044 7
architectural decoration	729.6
biochemistry	572.51
humans	612.015 24
building construction	693.7
building materials	691.8
chemistry	546.3
decorative arts	739
dowsing	133.323 3
economic geology	553.4
foundation materials	624.153 6
handicrafts	745.56
human toxicology	615.925 3
materials science	620.16
metabolism	572.514
human physiology	612.392 4
metallography	669.95
military resources	355.242
mineralogy	549.23
mining	622.34

and so on.

Notation

DDC notation uses only Arabic numerals. Use of only one type of symbol is called pure notation. All numbers contain at least three digits. Where more than three digits are needed, a decimal point follows the third digit.

In the print version of DDC, numbers are written in groups of three digits, with a space between each group—e.g., 344.063 635 1. This is done only to make writing and remembering numbers easier.

Some notation is mnemonic—that is, it is easy to remember some numbers because they are used consistently for a particular topic or subtopic. For example, 9 often represents geography or history, whether in the class 900 (Geography and history), or in the standard subdivision -09 (Historical, geographic, persons treatment).

Segmentation and Reduction

DDC allows for numbers to be reduced if the library requires a shorter number. Some copy cataloging sources, including cataloging-in-publication, show the segmentation of DDC numbers to enable shorter numbers to be identified easily. For example, 025.4'31 means that 025.431 is the complete number, but 025.4 is also correct (although less specific).

If segmentation is not shown, you need to consult the schedules to find a meaningful reduced number. As you develop familiarity with DDC, reduction will often be possible without needing to consult the schedules.

Advantages of DDC

1. DDC was the first classification scheme to use the concept of relative location to organize materials on the shelf.
2. The pure notation (i.e., all Arabic numbers) is recognized internationally.
3. The straightforward numerical sequence facilitates filing and shelving.
4. The Relative Index brings together different aspects of the same subject which are scattered in different disciplines.
5. The hierarchical notation expresses the relationship between and among class numbers.
6. The decimal system enables infinite expansion and subdivision.
7. The mnemonic notation helps users to memorize and recognize class numbers.
8. Periodic revision keeps it up-to-date.

Disadvantages of DDC

1. Its Anglo-American bias is evident in its emphasis on American, English, and European language, literature, and history in the 400s, 800s, and 900s, and Protestantism/Christianity in the 200s.
2. Some related disciplines are separated: e.g., 400 and 800; 300 and 900.

3. Some subjects are not very comfortably placed:

> e.g., Library science in 000
>
>> Psychology as part of Philosophy in 100
>>
>> Sports and amusements in 700.

4. In the 800s, literary works by the same author are scattered according to form:

> e.g., Shakespeare's poems are separated from his plays.

5. Decimal numbering limits its capacity for accommodating subjects on the same level because there can only be 9 divisions (+ 1 general division).

6. Different rates of growth of some disciplines have resulted in an uneven structure:

> e.g., 300 and 600 are particularly overcrowded.

7. Although theoretically expansion is infinite, it doesn't allow infinite insertion between related numbers, e.g., between 610 and 619.

8. Specificity results in long numbers, which can be awkward for shelving and on spine labels.

9. Altering numbers because of a new edition creates practical problems in libraries:

> e.g., the need for reclassification, relabeling, and reshelving.

Order of DDC Numbers

DDC numbers are arranged in decimal number order. In other words, after the decimal point, look at each decimal place one at a time and put those numbers in order. Unless they are the same, you will not need to look at the next place.

For example:

    348.003
    348.01
    348.02
    348.022
    348.04
    348.041
    348.6
    348.74
    348.744

EXERCISE 2.1

Check the order of these numbers, and correct them where necessary:

616	361
616.11	361.1
616.122	361.02
616.123	361.04
616.125	361.003
616.1237	361.103
616.091	361.2
616.24	361.3
616.201	361.23
616.241	361.301
616.244	361.32
616.200475	361.322
616.2009	361.323
616.240083	361.37
615.954	361.32305
617.44	361.3703
617.80083	361.37025
617.08	361.3205
617.0083	361.320994

REVIEW QUIZ 2.2

Use the following questions to revise your understanding of the structure of DDC. You do not need to write down the answers.

1.   Describe the overall structure of Dewey Decimal Classification.

2.   What is the purpose of the First, Second and Third Summaries? When would you use them?

3.   Why is the Relative Index so called?

4.   Give three advantages of DDC.

5.   Give three disadvantages of DDC.

Chapter 3
PRINCIPLES OF CLASSIFYING WITH DDC

Introduction
The introduction in Volume 1 outlines a number of principles of classifying with Dewey Decimal Classification. The most significant principles are summarized here. It is important to read the introduction and to refer to it from time to time.

Basic Principles of Classification
1. Place a work where it will be most useful.
   Classification must take into account the needs of the users, for example, in how specific a number is given.

2. Class a work according to the author's intent.
   A book of drawings of dogs may be classified with drawing or with dogs, depending on whether it is intended as a guide to drawing dogs or to identifying breeds of dog.

3. Class by subject, then by form, except in works of the imagination.
   An encyclopedia of art is classified with art rather than general encyclopedias.

4. In works of the imagination, class by original language, then literary form, rather than by subject.
   An anthology of English-language poems about the weather is classified with English poetry, not meteorology; a French translation of an English play is classified with English drama.

5. Class a work in the most specific area possible.
   A work about violins is classified at the specific number for violins rather than the more general number for stringed instruments.

6. Class a work which covers two or more subjects with the one that receives fuller treatment.
   A work about airplanes with a chapter on space shuttles is classified at the number for aircraft.

7. If a work includes two subjects in the same discipline which receive equal treatment and are not used to introduce or explain one another, class the work with the subject coming first in the schedules.
   A work on physics and chemistry is classified at the number for physics, since it comes first in the schedules.

8. If a work treats two aspects of a subject in different disciplines, class the work at the interdisciplinary number if one is given (provided the work contains significant material on that discipline).
   A work on music in education and religious worship is classified at the interdisciplinary number for music.

9. If no emphasis is apparent, class a work on three or more subjects that are all subdivisions of a broader subject with the first higher number which includes them all.
   A work on arithmetic, algebra, and calculus is classified at the number for mathematics.

10. Class a work on three or more subjects in different disciplines in the generalities class.
    A work on history, geography, economics, and politics is classified in 000 Generalities.

11. Class biographies, autobiographies, diaries and reminiscences either with specific disciplines or together in a general biography section.
    In a technical library, the life of an inventor is classified with the invention, whereas in a public library all kinds of biographies may be located together.

12. In general, class a work first by subject then by geographical location.
    A work on German architecture is classified first at the number for architecture.

13. When there is a further subdivision and there is a choice between subject and geographical location, choose the subject first.
    For a work on the architecture of German school buildings, the number for the architecture of school buildings is assigned before adding a number for Germany.

14. If a subject acts upon another subject, class it under the subject which is acted upon.
    A work on decoration in architecture is classified in architecture.

15. If a work has been treated from a particular standpoint, class it in the subject unless it has been considerably altered.
    Mathematics for plumbers is classified at the number for mathematics.

16. Works on topics "with special reference to" are classed under the more specific subject.
    A work on contagious diseases, especially leprosy, is classified at the number for leprosy.

17. When a subject has no stated place in the classification scheme, use the number of the subject to which it is most closely related.
    For advertising on the Internet, use the number for advertising using particular media.

18. When two headings clash, decide which is to prevail, and be consistent in its use.
    For political and armed struggle in Ireland, decide between politics and military science in Ireland.

19. Works pro and con a subject go together at the subject.
    Works for and against voluntary euthanasia must be found at the same number—this reinforces the principle of objectivity in the library's collection.

20. Avoid placings which are in the nature of criticism.
    Do not place works on prostitution with law or ethics unless they specifically treat legal or ethical issues.

21. Always have a reason for your placing of a work.
    You need to know why you assign a particular number.

22. Record all decisions.
    Decisions about classification numbers may need to be referred to, to ensure consistent placement of similar works.

23. Read the introduction to the classification scheme.
    It is important to understand the approach of those who have created and maintain the scheme.

24. Check the number in the shelf list or catalog.
    This will assist in placing like works together.

EXERCISE 3.1

Using the above guidelines, name the subject at which you would classify the following titles, and which principle(s) you have used:

1.   Epilepsy is not a dirty word _____

2.   Conversations on drawing, painting and sculpture _____

3.   Astrology and your child _____

4.   The Miami Herald fishing and boating guide _____

5.   Society in view: a graphic atlas for the social sciences _____

6.   Kiiroi nezumi, by Hisashi Inoue (Japanese novelist, 1946-) _____

7.   Enquire within for everything _____

8.   Around Seattle: including the shores of Puget Sound (more than half the text deals with Seattle) _____

9.   Words on wine: quotations from world literature _____

10. Seven cities of Australia _____

11. The authority and relevance of the Bible in the modern world _____

12. Inflation in Bolivia _____

13. Apples and pears _____

14. The story of the apple _____

15. Apples, oranges, pears and plums _____

16. Peaches, nectarines and plums _____

17. Mechanical harvesting of berry fruit _____

18.   Treasury of Canadian landscape painting   _____

19.   North American guide to compost gardening with detailed
      instructions on composting   _____

20.   Keeping faith alive today   _____

Classifying with DDC

"Classifying a work with the DDC requires determination of the subject, the disciplinary focus, and, if applicable, the approach or form" (DDC introduction, paragraph 5.1).

Determining the Subject

The classifier needs to examine the work in hand. This examination includes:

- the title—sometimes not very helpful
- the rest of the title information—often much more informative
- the table of contents / chapter headings / subheadings—good indications of the main topics
- the preface / introduction / foreword—usually state the author's purpose
- scanning the text—confirms or alters your ideas about the subject
- cataloging-in-publication—can be useful, but take care, since it was prepared before the work was published.

If you are unfamiliar with the subject, you may need to consult a subject expert. Very occasionally it is necessary to consult reference works or reviews.

Determining the Discipline

Once you have decided on the subject of the work, choose the discipline in which the subject belongs. For example, if the work is about horses, decide whether it belongs with zoology in natural sciences (if it is about the anatomy and physiology of horses) or animal husbandry in applied sciences (if it is about breeding and rearing horses).

Then you can choose to look first in the Relative Index or go straight to the schedules. Many experienced classifiers turn to the schedules, but while you are learning the structure of DDC, it is usually easier to look up the terms in the Relative Index. The Relative Index offers several numbers for most terms, so your decision about the discipline is important in helping to identify the most likely number. It is still necessary to check the number in the schedules before making the final decision. Never use a classification number direct from the Relative Index without also checking the schedules.

Broad and Close Classification

Broad classification uses the main divisions and subdivisions of a scheme without breaking down into narrower concepts.

Close classification means classifying each work as specifically as possible, using all available subdivisions in the classification scheme.

EXERCISE 3.2

Is the classification of each subject broad or close?

Subject	Classification Heading	Broad / Close
Family therapy	Family therapy	_____
Marital relationship	Marriage & family	_____
Atlanta's history	History of Georgia	_____
Marriage counseling	Family problems & services	_____
Business mathematics	Mathematics	_____
Modern Spanish Bible	Modern language Bibles	_____
The Shakers (religious group)	Adherents of religious groups	_____
Blood	Blood	_____
Banking in Mexico	Mexican banks & banking	_____
Christian Church's views on sex, marriage & family	Christian attitudes on sex, marriage & family	_____

Citation and Preference Order

When a number of aspects (or characteristics or facets) of a subject (e.g., age, gender, place, historical period) need to be considered, citation and preference order give guidelines as to the order in which to deal with them.

Citation Order

Citation order applies when you are allowed to add two or more characteristics when building a number. It is the order in which you are instructed to add aspects of the subject, and is clearly specified in the number-building instruction. For example,

> Add to base number 647.94 notation 3-9 from Table 2, e.g. multiple dwellings for transients in Canada 647.9471; then add further as follows:
>
> ...
> 01   Hotels, inns, resorts
> 02   Motels
> 03   Bed and breakfast establishments
> ...

In other words, the citation order is
subject   +   place   +   specific category of subject.

Preference Order

When a subject has more than one characteristic but the rules allow only one to be added, the classifier needs to choose. Preference notes provide guidance; for example,

> Except where instructed otherwise, give preference first to ethnic group, second to nationality, last to basic races, e.g. ...

There are also preference tables. For example,

> 371.91 Education of students with physical disabilities
>
> > Unless other instructions are given, observe the following table of preference:
> >
> > | | |
> > |---|---|
> > | Students with linguistic disorders | 371.914 |
> > | Students with mobility impairments | 371.916 |
> > | Students with blindness & visual impairments | 371.911 |
> > | Students with hearing impairments | 371.912 |

That is, a work on the education of blind and deaf students is classified at 371.911, not 371.912. However, the education of paraplegic blind students is classified at 371.916, not 371.911.

Notes indicating citation and preference order can be found throughout the schedules and tables. It is very important to read all instructions in the sections you are consulting.

Call Numbers

A call number is the number on a library item which shows where it is located. It usually consists of a classification number, a book number and often a location symbol. For example,

REF	location symbol
636.7	classification number
HEW	book number

The classification number indicates the subject of the work and sometimes also the bibliographic form.

The book number relates to the item itself. It is usually taken from the author or the title of the item.

The location symbol shows where the item is housed. For example, a reference work may have "R" or "REF"; an audiovisual item may have "AV". Location symbols may also indicate a branch of a library system.

Classification Numbers

In DDC, the classification number is taken straight from the schedules or built according to instructions. It can be used with any type of book number. Since call numbers usually have to fit on the spine of the books, some libraries limit the length of the classification number for convenience.

Book Numbers

There are many types of book number. They include:
- a running number for each work at one classification number

e.g., 625.1	625.1	625.1	625.2
1	2	3	1

This is easy to apply, but does not arrange the works in alphabetical order of author, and separates different editions of the same title.

- the first three (sometimes four) letters of the author's surname, or the title if there is no author (in other words, main entry)

e.g., 625.1	625.1	625.1	625.2
MAC	MAC	MAD	BAT

This is also easy to apply and arranges the works in alphabetical order of main entry, but results in some call numbers being identical.

- the first three (sometimes four) letters of the author's surname, or the title, followed by a number to make each call number unique

e.g., 625.1	625.1	625.1	625.2
MAC	MAC.1	MAD	BAT

This arranges the works in approximate alphabetical order of main entry, but more care needs to be taken in allocating the book numbers so as not to duplicate them.

- a Cutter-Sanborn number (also called a Cutter number) taken from the Cutter-Sanborn three-figure author table. This table enables a library to have a unique call number for every item, while maintaining alphabetical arrangement by main entry.

e.g., 625.1	625.1	625.1	625.2
M118	M135	M179	B329

This arranges the works in alphabetical order of main entry, but it requires use of the Table and care needs to be taken to allocate book numbers correctly. Detailed instructions on how to create these numbers are included in the Cutter-Sanborn Table.

Biographies

It is common for the book number for biographies to be taken from the subject of the biography, rather than the author. A second symbol is sometimes added to represent the author's surname.

Shelf Listing

A shelf list is the record of the works in a library. Items in the shelf list are arranged in the same order as the works on the shelves.

Before automation, one card from each set of catalog cards was filed in the shelf list, which was accessible only to library staff. It was used:
- to guide classifiers as to the use of a particular number
- to check the most recent allocation of book numbers if the library used unique call numbers
- to show classifiers which numbers were used previously, to maintain consistency
- as an aid to collection development, to show the strengths, weaknesses, and gaps in the collection
- as an inventory record for stocktaking
- as a historical and statistical record of the collection
- as an insurance record
- to provide subject bibliographies for reference staff.

Almost all these functions can be performed by the automated catalog, and increasingly libraries do not maintain a separate shelf list:
- The need for a unique call number is reduced, since in most automated systems the circulation records are controlled by a separate barcode.
- Stocktaking (where it still occurs) is done by reading the barcodes on the items with a wand and using the automated system to compare this information with its database.
- Classification numbers can be checked direct from the catalog.
- Subject bibliographies can be produced by the system.
- In an automated system, each item has only one record with several access points, compared with the several cards for each item in a card catalog. Therefore the catalog is an accurate historical and statistical record and inventory, provided that it is backed up regularly and a backup copy is stored off-site.

Where automated libraries do have a separate shelf list, consideration must be given to its usefulness, compared with the cost of maintaining it.

REVIEW QUIZ 3.3

Use the following questions to revise your understanding of the principles of classifying with DDC. You do not need to write down the answers.

1. How much of a work do you need to examine to determine its subject?

2. Why is it important to decide the discipline?

3. Describe the difference between broad and close classification. Give an example.

4. What is citation order? What is preference order? Are they the same?

5. What does a call number consist of, and what is its purpose?

6. List three functions of a traditional shelf list which can be performed by an online catalog.

Chapter 4
COMPONENTS OF THE DEWEY DECIMAL CLASSIFICATION

Introduction

Volume 1 of DDC provides an introduction which explains quite simply the principles, structure and operation of the Classification. Much of it can be read immediately. Leave the sections you find too technical until you have begun to use DDC, and then try again—you will find it all makes sense once you have developed an understanding of the scheme.

Glossary

Volume 1 also contains a glossary of technical terms.

Overview—The Summaries

Ten Main Classes

Dewey Decimal Classification is designed to encompass all knowledge, dividing it into ten very broad classes—one for generalities and nine for subject disciplines. This is called the first summary. You may find it useful to memorize it, since knowing the overall structure will help you to use the scheme more effectively.

The summaries can be found at the front of Volume 2.

The first summary lists the ten classes, as shown below:

First Summary
The Ten Main Classes

000	**Generalities**
100	**Philosophy & psychology**
200	**Religion**
300	**Social sciences**
400	**Language**
500	**Natural sciences & mathematics**
600	**Technology (Applied sciences)**
700	**The arts Fine and decorative arts**
800	**Literature & rhetoric**
900	**Geography & history**

EXERCISE 4.1

Once you have identified the subject of a work, you need to place it in one or another of these ten classes.

For example,

subject	discipline	class
logic	philosophy	100
Buddhism	religion	200
economics	social sciences	300
Latin grammar	language	400
chemistry	natural science	500
engineering	technology	600
sculpture	the arts	700
poetry	literature	800
history of Indonesia	history	900

Write the class number for each of the following:

1.   My book of opera

2.   A child's Bible

3.   Three Irish plays

4.   World Book encyclopedia

5.   Teach yourself Vietnamese

6.   The psychology of violence

7.   Russian rockets

8.   Physics for beginners

9.   Road atlas of New Zealand

10.   Employment of aged persons

11.   Multicultural education

12.   Encyclopaedia of Papua New Guinea

13.   How to draw cartoons

14.   Introductory philosophy

15.   Agricultural pest control

The Hundred Divisions

Each class is divided into ten divisions. Each division represents a part of the discipline. This is the second summary.

Second Summary*
The Hundred Divisions

000	**Generalities**		**500**	**Natural sciences & mathematics**
010	Bibliography		510	Mathematics
020	Library & information sciences		520	Astronomy & allied sciences
030	General encyclopedic works		530	Physics
040			540	Chemistry & allied sciences
050	General serial publications		550	Earth sciences
060	General organizations & museology		560	Paleontology Paleozoology
070	News media, journalism, publishing		570	Life sciences Biology
080	General collections		580	Plants
090	Manuscripts & rare books		590	Animals
100	**Philosophy & psychology**		**600**	**Technology (Applied sciences)**
110	Metaphysics		610	Medical sciences Medicine
120	Epistemology, causation, humankind		620	Engineering & allied operations
130	Paranormal phenomena		630	Agriculture & related technologies
140	Specific philosophical schools		640	Home economics & family living
150	Psychology		650	Management & auxiliary services
160	Logic		660	Chemical engineering
170	Ethics (Moral philosophy)		670	Manufacturing
180	Ancient, medieval, Oriental philosophy		680	Manufacture for specific uses
190	Modern western philosophy		690	Buildings
200	**Religion**		**700**	**The arts Fine and decorative arts**
210	Philosophy & theory of religion		710	Civic & landscape art
220	Bible		720	Architecture
230	Christianity Christian theology		730	Plastic arts Sculpture
240	Christian moral & devotional theology		740	Drawing & decorative arts
250	Christian orders & local church		750	Painting & paintings
260	Social & ecclesiastical theology		760	Graphic arts Printmaking & prints
270	History of Christianity & Christian church		770	Photography & photographs
280	Christian denominations & sects		780	Music
290	Comparative religion & other religions		790	Recreational & performing arts
300	**Social sciences**		**800**	**Literature & rhetoric**
310	Collections of general statistics		810	American literature in English
320	Political science		820	English & Old English literatures
330	Economics		830	Literatures of Germanic languages
340	Law		840	Literatures of Romance languages
350	Public administration & military science		850	Italian, Romanian, Rhaeto-Romanic
360	Social problems & services; association		860	Spanish & Portuguese literatures
370	Education		870	Italic literatures Latin
380	Commerce, communications, transportation		880	Hellenic literatures Classical Greek
390	Customs, etiquette, folklore		890	Literatures of other languages
400	**Language**		**900**	**Geography & history**
410	Linguistics		910	Geography & travel
420	English & Old English		920	Biography, genealogy, insignia
430	Germanic languages German		930	History of ancient world to ca. 499
440	Romance languages French		940	General history of Europe
450	Italian, Romanian, Rhaeto-Romanic		950	General history of Asia Far East
460	Spanish & Portuguese languages		960	General history of Africa
470	Italic languages Latin		970	General history of North America
480	Hellenic languages Classical Greek		980	General history of South America
490	Other languages		990	General history of other areas

*Consult schedules for complete and exact headings

EXERCISE 4.2

Using the second summary, write down the number of the division in which each of the following topics belongs. First decide the class, then the division.

1. Audiovisual materials in libraries   _____

2. Japanese printmaking   _____

3. Growing wheat for export   _____

4. Twentieth-century architecture   _____

5. A concise history of Chile   _____

6. The nursing handbook   _____

7. Paleontological studies   _____

8. Women into politics   _____

9. A historical atlas of ancient Egypt   _____

10. Carnivorous plants   _____

11. The Methodist Church in the Pacific   _____

12. Abortion   _____

13. The planet Mars   _____

14. How to play hockey   _____

15. Learn Polish: an audiovisual approach   _____

16. The Oxford English dictionary   _____

17. Caring for rare books   _____

18. Child psychology   _____

19. The legal handbook   _____

20. Jewish folktales   _____

The Thousand Sections
Each division is divided into ten sections. Each section is a whole number which represents a topic. This is the third summary.

It is useful to spend some time looking through the third summary, since it provides a more detailed overview of the content of the Dewey Decimal Classification. However, in order to locate classification numbers, you need to refer to the schedules, usually via the Relative Index.

Here is part of the third summary:

Social sciences

300	**Social sciences**
301	Sociology & anthropology
302	Social interaction
303	Social processes
304	Factors affecting social behavior
305	Social groups
306	Culture & institutions
307	Communities
308	
309	
310	**Collections of general statistics**
311	
312	
313	
314	General statistics of Europe
315	General statistics of Asia
316	General statistics of Africa
317	General statistics of North America
318	General statistics of South America
319	General statistics of other areas
320	**Political science**
321	Systems of governments & states
322	Relation of state to organized groups
323	Civil & political rights
324	The political process
325	International migration & colonization
326	Slavery & emancipation
327	International relations
328	The legislative process
329	
330	**Economics**
331	Labor economics
332	Financial economics
333	Economics of land & energy
334	Cooperatives
335	Socialism & related systems
336	Public finance
337	International economics
338	Production
339	Macroeconomics & related topics
340	**Law**
341	International law
342	Constitutional & administrative law
343	Military, tax, trade, industrial law
344	Labor, social, education, cultural law
345	Criminal law
346	Private law
347	Civil procedure & courts
348	Law (Statutes), regulations, cases
349	Law of specific jurisdictions & areas
350	**Public administration & military science**
351	Public administration
352	General considerations
353	Specific fields of public administration
354	Administration of economy & environment
355	Military science
356	Foot forces & warfare
357	Mounted forces & warfare
358	Air & other specialized forces
359	Sea (Naval) forces & warfare
360	**Social problems & services; association**
361	General social problems & welfare
362	Social welfare problems & services
363	Other social problems & services
364	Criminology
365	Penal & related institutions
366	Associations
367	General clubs
368	Insurance
369	Miscellaneous kinds of associations
370	**Education**
371	Schools & activities; special education
372	Elementary education
373	Secondary education
374	Adult education
375	Curricula
376	
377	
378	Higher education
379	Public policy issues in education
380	**Commerce, communications, transportation**
381	Internal commerce (Domestic trade)
382	International commerce (Foreign trade)
383	Postal communication
384	Communications Telecommunication
385	Railroad transportation
386	Inland waterway & ferry transportation
387	Water, air, space transportation
388	Transportation Ground transportation
389	Metrology & standardization
390	**Customs, etiquette, folklore**
391	Costume & personal appearance
392	Customs of life cycle & domestic life
393	Death customs
394	General customs
395	Etiquette (Manners)
396	
397	
398	Folklore
399	Customs of war & diplomacy

EXERCISE 4.3

Using the third summary, decide the section in which each of the following titles belongs. First decide the class, then the division, then look for the section.

1.   Developing educational curricula   _____

2.   Harrap's new German grammar   _____

3.   The plays of William Shakespeare   _____

4.   Electricity   _____

5.   Let's visit Kenya   _____

6.   The philosophy of Socrates   _____

7.   Southeast Asian cooking   .   _____

8.   What bird is that?   _____

9.   Journalism in the new Russia   _____

10. Steam trains for enthusiasts   _____

11. Islam   _____

12. Introduction to trout fishing   _____

The Schedules

Introduction

The schedules provide a systematic breakdown of the main classes, their divisions and their sections. More than 23,000 numbers are listed in a straight numerical sequence from 000 to 999. In addition, numbers can be made by using the number-building features of DDC, which are treated in Chapters 7-12.

The principle of hierarchy which governs the scheme means:

broad numbers—broad subjects		specific numbers—specific subjects	
e.g.,			
500	science	551.6365	long-range weather forecasting
780	music	787.8719366	techniques for playing the guitar left-handed

In general, the longer the DDC number, the more specific is the subject it represents.

Hierarchy in the Schedules

In the overall hierarchy of DDC the ten classes are divided into 100 divisions and 1,000 sections. Each division is a specific aspect of its main class, and (almost) every section is a specific aspect of the division in which it is found.

For example,

within	900	Geography and history
we find	930	History of ancient world

within	930	History of ancient world
we find	938	Greece (history of ancient)

This principle extends into the schedules.

For example,

900	Geography and history
930	History of ancient world to ca. 499
938	Greece to 323 (history of)
938.03	Persian Wars, 500-479 B.C. (part of the history of Greece to 323)

Here each topic within 900 (Geography and history) is a more specific aspect of the subject above it.

In this example, 938.03 is described as subordinate to 938; 938 is superordinate to 938.03.

EXERCISE 4.4

Using the above example, complete the following:

1. 900 is superordinate to _____.

2. 930 is _____ to 900.

3. _____ is subordinate to 938.

Layout of the Hierarchical Structure

The layout of the schedules shows the hierarchy both by type size and by indentation. Here is the same hierarchy again as printed in the schedules, showing clearly the subordination of the more specific numbers:

900 Geography and history

930	**History of ancient world to ca. 499**
938	**Greece to 323**
938.03	Persian Wars, 500-479 B.C.

As you read the subordinate numbers, remember to include the superordinate headings above, since they are not always repeated for each more specific topic.

The Tables

DDC contains seven auxiliary tables, which are used to build more specific numbers than are listed in the schedules.

For example, for almost every topic, it may be necessary to add a geographic aspect—e.g., there may be works on trade unionism in most places. So that the schedules do not have to list each topic for every place, the scheme allows a constant number for a place to be added to the number for almost any topic. The numbers for geographic places are found in a table.

In the same way, there are dictionaries or encyclopedias of many subjects. DDC allows the classifier to construct a specific number for a dictionary of religion by adding to the schedule number for religion a number from a table which represents dictionaries.

The tables are:
Table 1	Standard subdivisions
Table 2	Geographic areas, historical periods, persons
Table 3	Subdivisions for the arts, for individual literatures, for specific literary forms
Table 4	Subdivisions of individual languages and language families
Table 5	Racial, ethnic, national groups
Table 6	Languages
Table 7	Groups of persons

Numbers in the tables are intended to be used only with numbers from the schedules, never alone. They are always quoted as T1-, T2-, T3-, etc., to show that they are added to an existing classification number.

The tables follow the introduction in Volume 1. Numbers can only be added from the tables by following particular rules. The tables are treated in Chapters 7-11.

The Relative Index

The Relative Index relates subjects to the disciplines of which they are part. The subjects are arranged alphabetically showing the disciplines in which they are treated.

For example,
Computers	004
access control	005.8
management	658.478
elementary education	374.34
engineering	621.39
instructional use	371.334
adult level	374.26
elementary level	372.133 4
law	343.099 9
music	780.285
composition	781.34
musical instruments	786.76
social effects	303.483 4

The first number given (004) is the interdisciplinary number for a work on computers. Listed below the heading are alternative numbers for computers, depending on the discipline in which they belong or the aspect of the subject being emphasized.

It is important to decide on the class before consulting the Relative Index. Then the class will help locate the best number for the subject.

For example, the electronic performance of computers belongs in Technology (600s). Look at the index entry above. There are only two numbers in the 600s—one in the 620s (Engineering) and one in the 650s (Management). So the number 621.39 seems the best choice.

Terms in the Relative Index

The following are included in the Relative Index:
- terms found in the headings and notes of the schedules
- synonyms
- selected terms in common use
- names of countries, their states and provinces
- names of counties in the U.S.
- names of capital cities and other important municipalities
- names of certain important geographical features, e.g., Pacific Ocean
- heads of state used to identify historical periods, e.g., Louis XIV
- founders of religion, e.g., Muhammad
- initiators of schools of thought, e.g., Adam Smith.

Place names and proper names should be in *AACR2 (Anglo-American cataloguing rules 2nd edition)* format.

The following are *not* included in the Relative Index:
- phrases beginning with the adjective form of languages and countries, e.g., American short stories, French cooking
- phrases containing general concepts represented by standard subdivisions such as education, statistics, laboratories and management, e.g., art education, educational statistics

The Relative Index is found in Volume 4.

The Manual

The Manual gives advice about how to classify difficult topics, especially where it may be hard to choose between two possible numbers. It also provides detailed information about revisions to the scheme and explains the policies and practices of the Decimal Classification Division at the Library of Congress.

For example, building and architecture are in different places in the classification scheme (Building is in the 600s; Architecture is in the 700s). It is sometimes difficult to decide where some works about buildings and building design belong. The relevant parts of the schedules, 690.1 and 721, refer to the Manual: *See Manual at 721 vs. 690.1*. The Manual at *721 vs. 690.1* explains the specific uses of each number and concludes "If in doubt, prefer 721".

It is very useful to consult the Manual when assistance or more information is needed. It follows the Relative Index in Volume 4.

REVIEW QUIZ 4.5

Use the following questions to revise your understanding of the components of DDC. You do not need to write down the answers.

1. What is the importance of disciplines in the Dewey Decimal Classification?

2. What is hierarchy in DDC and why is it important?

3. In the hierarchy   150   Psychology
                     155   Differential and developmental pyschology
                     155.4   Child pyschology
    is 155 superordinate to, coordinate with, or subordinate to 155.4? What does this mean?

4. If a DDC number is very long, is it more likely to be a specific number or a broad number? Why?

5. What is the role of the auxiliary tables?

6. Does the index contain all the subjects listed in the schedules?

7. Why is it called the Relative Index?

8. In this excerpt from the Relative Index, what is the interdisciplinary number for helicopters?

Helicopters	387.733 52
engineering	629.133 352
military engineering	623.746 047
piloting	629.132 525 2
transportation services	387.733 52

9. Where would you look for a comparison of the use of 550 (Earth sciences) and 910 (Geography and travel)?

10. Where in DDC will you find a definition of the "rule of three"? What is it?

Chapter 5
FINDING A NUMBER IN THE SCHEDULES

Introduction

To classify a work, first determine the subject, then the discipline to which the subject belongs.

It is also important to consider the nature of the collection and its users and whether there are any library policies (e.g., location of particular items, level of specificity, maximum number of digits) which may affect the classification.

Specific Aspects of a Subject

As well as a whole subject being more or less specific, aspects or facets of a subject can be more or less important. For example, to classify the topic "Breeding horses in Montana in the 1970s", you must identify the main subject and each of the aspects of the subject.

In this example:

Main subject:	Breeding horses
Secondary aspect:	in Montana
Secondary aspect:	in the 1970s.

Some classification numbers will allow you to include both secondary aspects of the subject and others will not. Sometimes, you will have to decide which of the secondary aspects is more important. Sometimes the citation or preference order makes this decision.

EXERCISE 5.1

For the following titles, identify the main subject and as many secondary aspects of the subject (in any order) as you think there are.

1.   An illustrated history of 15th century Japan

Main subject: _____

Secondary aspect: _____

Secondary aspect: _____

2.   A dictionary of terms for motorists

Main subject: _____

Secondary aspect: _____

3.   The history of glass-blowing in Venice in the Middle Ages

Main subject: _____

Secondary aspect: _____

Secondary aspect: _____

Secondary aspect: _____

Begin with the Class

Since the classes govern the overall structure, once you have decided what the work is about, determine the class in which the main subject belongs.

Next, identify all the secondary aspects of the work and then the importance of each of these aspects.

For example,

    Censorship in Iran: an encyclopedia

Main subject:	Censorship
Discipline (class):	Social sciences (300)
Secondary aspects:	Iran
	Encyclopedia
Order of importance:	1 - Censorship
	2 - Iran
	3 - Encyclopedia

Looking for DDC Numbers: A Summary

1. Determine:
   i. subject
   ii. discipline (class)
   iii.   significant parts of the subject
   iv. significant order of the parts.

2. Look up the subject in the index, choosing the number that corresponds to the discipline.

3. Check the number in the schedules to ensure that
   i. it is correct
   ii. it is at the required level of specificity.

Note: Never classify directly from the index. Always check the schedules.

Searching the Relative Index

Once you have decided what the work is about, choose the most specific description of the subject. Always search the index first for the most specific term. If the term is not found, try a broader term.

Terms are arranged alphabetically, word by word. Terms are indented below the main heading. The DDC numbers are spaced at every third number after the decimal point; this is only for convenience of reading.

See also references are used for synonyms and for references to broader and related terms.

EXERCISE 5.2

Assign DDC numbers to each of the following subjects.
i.   Decide what the subject is.
ii. Decide which class it belongs to.
iii. Look in the index for as specific a topic as possible.
iv. Check the number in the schedules.

1.   Keyword indexing: an introduction to KWIC and KWOC

     Class _____   Specific term(s) _____

     DDC number _____

2.   Laws relating to the disposal of human remains

     Class _____   Specific term(s) _____

     DDC number _____

3.   Home care nursing

     Class _____   Specific term(s) _____

     DDC number _____

4.   Homosexuality—right or wrong?

     Class _____   Specific term(s) _____

     DDC number _____

5.   The twelve tribes of ancient Israel

     Class _____   Specific term(s) _____

     DDC number _____

6.   Build your house with adobe bricks

    Class   _____   Specific term(s)   _____

    DDC number   _____

7.   Blood banks—a public service

    Class   _____   Specific term(s)   _____

    DDC number   _____

8.   God in Islam

    Class   _____   Specific term(s)   _____

    DDC number   _____

9.   How volcanoes are formed

    Class   _____   Specific term(s)   _____

    DDC number   _____

10.   Family counseling

    Class   _____   Specific term(s)   _____

    DDC number   _____

11.   The psychology of perception

    Class   _____   Specific term(s)   _____

    DDC number   _____

12.   Ancient Chinese philosophy

    Class   _____   Specific term(s)   _____

    DDC number   _____

13.   Hazardous toys

    Class   _____   Specific term(s)   _____

    DDC number   _____

14.   Architecture of school buildings

     Class   _____   Specific term(s)   _____

     DDC number   _____

15.   The causes of World War II

     Class   _____   Specific term(s)   _____

     DDC number   _____

Chapter 6
ORGANIZATION OF THE SCHEDULES

Reading the Schedules

Reading the full number and its complete heading depends on understanding the principle of hierarchy.

Here is an extract from the schedules:

302   *Social sciences*

.2   Communication

.2223   Symbols

To read the whole number, include the number at the top of the page, since most of the entries only show the decimal portion. So,
.2223   Symbols
is not the whole number. Find the superordinate (whole) number 302 at the top of this page to read the number as 302.2223.

Similarly, the heading
.2223   Symbols
is not clear, until you read back up the hierarchy to the heading above:
.2   Communication

So, 302.2223 means Symbols of communication.

EXERCISE 6.1

DDC numbers are hierarchical. Here is an example of the hierarchy:

796.8309

700	The arts
790	Recreational and performing arts
796	Athletic and outdoor sports and games
796.8	Combat sports
796.83	Boxing
796.8309	History of boxing

Reconstruct these numbers in the same way, showing the hierarchy and including in each heading enough detail to identify the complete heading:

1.   345.072

2.   659.143

3.   375.001

4.   599.972

5.   910.452

Interpreting the Schedules

Here is another extract. Open Volume 2 at this section of the schedules and study it alongside the explanations below:

300 Social sciences

Class here behavioral studies, social studies	This is a **class-here** note which tells us what to use the number for
Class a specific behavioral science with the subject, e.g., psychology 150 ...	This is a **class-elsewhere** note, which refers us to a different number
For language, see 400; for history, see 900	These are **see references** which direct us to other locations for specific parts of the subject
See Manual at 300; also at 150; also at 300 vs. 600	This **see-Manual** note directs us to more detailed explanations in the Manual

SUMMARY

300.1-.9	Standard subdivisions
301	Sociology and anthropology
302	Social interaction
303	Social processes
304	Factors affecting social behavior
305	Social groups
306	Culture and institutions
307	Communities
...	

The many **summaries** of the coverage of a division or a number may help you find your way around

301	Sociology and anthropology
...	
[.019]	Psychological principles Do not use; class in 302

Square brackets are used when numbers are not to be used, because the number is not assigned, or has been relocated or discontinued

Options

Parentheses are used for optional numbers which may suit individual libraries but are not part of the standard notation.

For example, DDC recognizes that Christianity is not the main religion of many users of the Classification. So, at 291, it provides this option:

> (Option: To give preferred treatment or shorter numbers to a specific religion other than Christianity, class it in this number, and add to base number 291 the numbers following the base number for that religion in 292-299, e.g., Hinduism 291, Mahabharata 291.923 ... Other options are described at 292-299)

A few other optional numbers are also included, e.g.,

> (330.159) Socialist and related schools
> (Optional number; prefer 335)

Centered Entries

Many headings refer to a span of numbers rather than a single number. In these cases, the heading is printed in the center of the page and is marked by the symbol > in the number column.

For example,

> \>   **930-990   History of ancient world; of specific continents, countries, localities; of extraterrestrial worlds**

All instructions under this heading apply to all numbers in the range 930-990. This saves having to provide the same information separately for each number.

Other Notes

There are other notes in the schedules, most of which are self-explanatory.

It is very important to read the relevant section of the schedule, including checking the hierarchy and reading all the notes which apply to your number, as well as the superordinate numbers in the appropriate part of the hierarchy.

For example, when checking the number 693.22 (Building with adobe bricks), it is useful to read the notes at 693, 690.1, and 690. Also read the Manual entry at *721 vs. 690.1*, which is referred to under 690.1 (Structural elements).

EXERCISE 6.2

Find an example of each of these in the schedules. If you are not sure what a term means, check the glossary in Volume 1 of DDC or at the back of this book.

1.   A heading   _____

2.   A summary   _____

3.   A centered heading   _____

4.   A subordinate number   _____

5.   A relocated topic   _____

6.   A class-elsewhere note   _____

7.   A see-also reference   _____

8.   A see reference   _____

9.   A scope note   _____

10. An option   _____

EXERCISE 6.3

Which is the correct number in each of the following groups?
i.   Find each number in the schedules and identify the topic it represents
ii. Choose the number which most closely represents the subject given

1.   Sodium vapor lighting in public areas

     621.3276

     621.324

     628.95

2.   Decorative horn carving

     788.94

     681.8

     736.6

3. Gold in folklore

    398.3

    398.365

    549.23

    739.22

    553.41

4. Victims of crime

    364.44

    362.88

    363.23

    365.46

5. Household heating

    665.5384

    621.4025

    644.1

6. Prevention of heart disease

    616.12

    617.412

    641.56311

    614.5912

EXERCISE 6.4

Find DDC numbers for the following using the index and the schedules:

1. The history of the Punic Wars   _____

2. An introduction to photochemistry   _____

3. Big game hunting   _____

4. How valleys are formed   _____

5.   The Ouija board in spiritualism   _____

6.   The identification of waterbirds   _____

7.   How to read maps   _____

8.   The Lutheran Church in America   _____

9.   New ideas in tax reform   _____

10. Unemployment resulting from technological change   _____

11. Cycle racing   _____

12. Behavior of people in disasters   _____

13. Electricity from the wind   _____

14. Cleaning clothes at home   _____

15. Sculpture in wax and wood   _____

EXERCISE 6.5
Find DDC numbers for the following using the index and the schedules:

1.   Ethiopia under Italian rule   _____

2.   Drawing and preparing maps   _____

3.   Social responsibility of executive management   _____

4.   Talismans in witchcraft   _____

5.   Rules of Parliament   _____

6.   Detergent technology   _____

7.   Military intelligence   _____

8.   Ultrasonic vibrations   _____

9.   Design of roadworks   _____

10. Sculpture in the twentieth century   _____

11. Plant diseases   _____

12. Speed drills for typing   _____

13.   The ethics of government   _____

14.   Music for the guitar   _____

15.   Discipline in the classroom   _____

16.   Zodiac: an astrological guide   _____

17.   Making trousers commercially   _____

18.   Looking after your pet canary   _____

EXERCISE 6.6
Find DDC numbers for the following using the index and the schedules:

1.   An introduction to the violin and other bowed string instruments   _____

2.   Design and construction of clocks   _____

3.   Cookery in restaurants   _____

4.   How to code computer programs   _____

5.   The use of radio in adult education   _____

6.   Evolution of microbes   _____

7.   Growing carrots in the home garden   _____

8.   Techniques for indoor photography   _____

9.   Eighteenth-century sculpture   _____

10.   Manufacture of paper   _____

11.   Triplets, quads and more: an obstetric guide   _____

12.   The Panama Canal: modern aid to transportation   _____

13.   The physics of auroras   _____

14.   Flying fishes and seahorses: odd marine creatures   _____

15.   A guide to cooking with pressure cookers   _____

Chapter 7
NUMBER BUILDING AND
TABLE 1: STANDARD SUBDIVISIONS

Introduction
DDC began as an enumerative classification scheme. That is, all the numbers were listed, and the classifier simply looked them up. Over time, the scheme has provided for more numbers to be constructed (synthesized) by adding to a number in the schedules.

Numbers can be built by adding to a base number
- from a table
- from another part of the schedule.

Chapters 7-11 deal with the auxiliary tables. Adding from another part of the schedules is covered in Chapter 12.

The Auxiliary Tables
The auxiliary tables in DDC are intended to be used only with numbers from the schedules, never alone. They are always quoted as T1-, T2-, T3-, etc., to show that they are added to an existing classification number. There are seven auxiliary tables:

Table 1   Standard subdivisions
Table 2   Geographic areas, historical periods, persons
Table 3   Subdivisions for the arts, for individual literatures, for specific literary forms
Table 4   Subdivisions of individual languages and language families
Table 5   Racial, ethnic, national groups
Table 6   Languages
Table 7   Groups of persons

With the exception of the standard subdivisions, they are only to be added to a classification number when special instructions appear at that number.

Unless special instructions are given, only one number from an auxiliary table can be added to a classification number. If more than one applies to a work, there is a table of preference on page 4 of Volume 1, and the classifier must choose the number which appears first in that table.

Table 1: Standard Subdivisions
In nonfiction materials, there are some regular patterns of treatment. For example, in a subject such as Psychology, there are works which deal with:

Philosophy and theory of psychology
Research in psychology
History of psychology
Psychology as practiced in different parts of the world

In the same way, a subject may appear in a number of recognized forms, e.g.,

Serial	Illustrated
Directory	Dictionary
Tables or statistics	Encyclopedia

In DDC, these regularly recurring forms or treatments of a subject are recognized as "standard" methods. This allows a work to be classified at its main subject and added to by using numbers from Table 1.

No special instructions from the schedules are needed to add standard subdivisions. They can be added freely, when needed, to any classification number, although only one is added for any one work.

Useful standard subdivisions include:

-01 Philosophy and theory
-022 Illustrations, models, miniatures
-025 Directories of persons and organizations
-03 Dictionaries, encyclopedias, concordances
-05 Serial publications
-06 Organizations and management
-07 Education, research, related topics
-08 History and description with respect to kinds of persons
-09 Historical, geographic, persons treatment

The standard subdivision -09 is sometimes combined with numbers from Table 2, so that the geographic treatment can be linked to a specific country or location, e.g.,

	Number from schedules	364	Criminology
+	standard subdivision	-09	Geographical treatment
+	number from Table 2	-773 11	Chicago
	=	**364.0977311**	**Criminology in Chicago**

Purposes of Standard Subdivisions

Standard subdivisions are used
- to make a classification number more specific
- to distinguish between different ways of treating the subject
- to describe how a work is treated, so that items dealing with a "big" subject can be grouped together on the shelves, e.g.,

Brown	Smith
Theory of	Banking
banking	theory
332.101	332.101

As standard subdivisions begin with -0, DDC ensures that these "standard" treatments of the subject can be shelved in their groups before the subject is further subdivided in the tables, e.g.,

Brown	Smith	Adams	Carter
Theory of	History of	Commercial	Theory of
banking	banking	banks	commercial banks
332.101	332.109	332.12	332.120 1

If the schedules are already full at the -0 number, there are special directions on how to apply standard subdivisions at those numbers. Usually -001, -002, -003, etc., are used to keep the standard subdivisions at the beginning of the number for the topic.

Principles for Applying Standard Subdivisions

1. They must never be used alone, but only with a number from the schedules. This is why they are always quoted as T1-01, -03 etc. The dash is not used in the combined number; it simply shows that the number is incomplete.

2. The digits in the standard subdivisions may be applied to any base number. If the base number is less than 3 digits, combine it with the standard subdivisions number, and add the decimal point where necessary, e.g.,

Base number for technology	6 +	
Trademarks & service marks	-0275	
Trademarks & service marks of products	=	602.75

3. Do not add one standard subdivision to another, unless there are specific instructions to do so.

When Not to Use the Standard Subdivisions

Although standard subdivisions are applicable throughout the schedules, under some circumstances they should not be used:

- When the number is already built into the schedules (e.g., 501, 502, 503). Always check the classification number to see if this is the case. Do not try to add standard subdivisions to a number found in the index.

- When they would be redundant (i.e., if the base number already means safety measures, it would be unnecessary to add -0289—safety measures).

- When there is an instruction not to use the standard subdivisions.

- When the subject of the work is more specific than the classification number. For example, a work on Black widow spiders has to be classified at 595.44—Spiders, because there is no number that is more specific. In this case, don't add a standard subdivision. Many kinds of spiders will have to be grouped at this number, and in future editions of DDC new numbers may be developed to separate them. This space to add more specific numbers is called "standing room". Since any addition to the number now may conflict with a future expansion of the number, do not build further.

How to Add from Table 1

1. Identify the subject proper, and then the element(s) represented by standard subdivision(s).
2. Classify the subject proper using the Relative Index and checking in the schedules.
3. Find the notation you need for the standard subdivision, either using the Relative Index or directly from Table 1.
4. Check the schedules to see whether there are any instructions about standard subdivisions.
5. Add the table number to the schedule number.
6. Check the schedules again to ensure there is no conflict with a number or instruction.

For example,

Encyclopedia of international law			
International law	341 +		
Encyclopedia	-03	=	341.03
The terminology of stars			
Stars	523.8 +		
Terminology	-014	=	523.801 4
Civil engineering as a profession			
Civil engineering	624 +		
As a profession	-023	=	624.023

Programmed texts in algebra and number theory
    Algebra and number theory   512 +
    Programmed texts   -077
    But 512 (Algebra and number theory) has the instruction
      Use 512.001-512.009 for standard subdivisions
    So
    Programmed texts in algebra and number theory =   512.007 7

EXERCISE 7.1

Construct DDC numbers for the following topics, using the Relative Index, the schedules and Table 1.

1. Dictionary of child psychology   _____

2. Journal of manufacture of electronic toys   _____

3. The language of soccer   _____

4. Pony weekly   _____

5. Teaching netball   _____

6. The philosophy of idealism   _____

7. The philosophy of social work   _____

8.   Standards for lathes   _____

9.   Dictionary of biochemistry   _____

10.   A history of child care   _____

11.   Systems of long-range weather forecasting   _____

12.   Sales catalog of kitchen goods   _____

13.   Guidebook for a toy museum   _____

14.   The terrier encyclopedia   _____

15.   Genetics research   _____

16.   Handicrafts for people with disabilities   _____

EXERCISE 7.2

Look at the schedules and standard subdivisions in Table 1. Find the subject for each of the following numbers and supply a suitable title.

For example,
658.008 694 1—Management skills for the unemployed

1.   796.352 05   _____

2.   370.3   _____

3.   371.003   _____

4.   372.03   _____

5.   375.000 3   _____

6.   629.132 300 5   _____

7.   181.005   _____

8.   336.002 85   _____

9.   621.388 007 2   _____

10.   730.74   _____

11.   300.724   _____

12. 512.005 _____

13. 512.705 _____

14. 338.430 007 2 _____

"Nonstandard" Addition of Standard Subdivisions

As you have seen in the last exercise, there are many places in the schedules where you cannot simply add the notation -01, etc., to the number in the schedule. These include:

- main classes
- divisions
- some other numbers indicated in the schedules.

It is necessary to check the schedules, where most irregular usage is indicated by an instruction,

e.g.,   SUMMARY

      540.1-.9   Standard subdivisions

or

      Use 335.001-335.009 for standard subdivisions

Also check the schedule for patterns. Where one standard subdivision is used in a particular way, the others follow the same pattern, unless otherwise instructed.

For example,

510   Mathematics
510.1   Philosophy and theory
The other standard subdivisions for Mathematics follow the same pattern, so Mathematics as a profession = 510.23

500   Natural sciences and mathematics
501   Philosophy and theory
502   Miscellany
These are the standard subdivisions, so follow the pattern for all of them.

375   Curricula
.0001-.0009   Standard subdivisions
This pattern requires extra zeroes.

Use of -04 for Special Topics

Some numbers in the schedules make use of the standard subdivision -04, which is reserved for special topics.

For example,
621 Applied physics
.04   Special topics
.042   Energy engineering
.044   Plasma engineering

Facet Indicators

In the notation -09, 0 is called a facet indicator. That is, its purpose is to indicate that a facet is being added to the number. Facet indicators are sometimes shown as part of the base number. For example, in 778.52 (General topics of cinematography and video production), 2 is added to the number 778.5 to introduce the special numbers for the facets of cinematography which follow.

EXERCISE 7.3

Assign DDC numbers to the following works, using the Relative Index, the schedules, and Table 1.

1.   Dictionary of library and information science   _____

2.   Philosophy of library science   _____

3.   Library and information science: a journal   _____

4.   Dictionary of psychology   _____

5.   Psychology: historical research   _____

6.   Dictionary of ethics   _____

7.   Ethics: a quarterly journal   _____

8.   Epidemiology: psychological principles   _____

9.   Dictionary of architecture   _____

10. Study and teaching of chemical technology   _____

EXERCISE 7.4

Assign DDC numbers to the following works, using the Relative Index, the schedules and Table 1.

1.   Popular engineering (quarterly journal)   _____

2.   Agricultural pest control index   _____

3. Techniques and apparatus used in puppetry _____

4. Correspondence courses in electronics _____

5. Cookery in the Middle Ages _____

6. Encyclopedia of horses _____

7. History of the social sciences _____

8. Philosophy of Christianity _____

9. Historical research into public administration _____

10. Lives of ten great artists _____

11. Theory of the solar system _____

12. Research in oceanography _____

13. Trotting monthly _____

14. Theory of personnel management _____

15. Book publishing trade catalogs _____

16. Journal of the philosophy of socialism _____
    (Hint: use the table of preference)

More Than One Standard Subdivision

Some works have more than one aspect of the main subject, each of which could be represented by a standard subdivision. However, the rules prohibit use of more than one standard subdivision in most cases.

First consider whether one standard subdivision is much more important in the subject than the other(s).

For example, in the subject Research in Japanese photography, there are two possible standard subdivisions: Research and Geographical treatment (Japan). The main subject is Japanese photography, so use the standard subdivision -09 to include the geographical aspect, and ignore the secondary aspect of research.

However, if the secondary aspects of the subject are of equal significance, refer to the table of preference at the beginning of Table 1. This shows which aspect of the subject to include.

For example, a journal of economic geology research has the main topic Economic geology and two possible standard subdivisions: Research and Serials. In the table of preference, -072 (Research) comes before -05 (Serial publications), so the completed number will be

Economic geology	+	research		
553	+	-072	=	553.072

REVIEW QUIZ 7.5

Use the following questions to revise your understanding of standard subdivisions. You do not need to write down the answers.

1. Why does DDC use standard subdivisions?

2. When can they be added?

3. How do you know that a number given in the Relative Index is a standard subdivision?

4. Are there situations in which standard subdivisions should not be used? What are they?

5. What do the following standard subdivisions stand for?

   -01 _____

   -03 _____

   -05 _____

   -07 _____

   -09 _____

6. Why do standard subdivisions begin with -0?

7. Why do you need to check the schedules when constructing a number using a standard subdivision?

8. 545 (Quantitative analysis) has the special instruction "Use 545.001-545.009 for standard subdivisions".
   What is the number for History of quantitative analysis?

9. What is the table of preference? When is it used?

10. Using the table of preference, which standard subdivision will you use for the topic Equipment and teaching in hydraulic engineering?

Chapter 8
TABLE 2: GEOGRAPHIC AREAS, HISTORICAL PERIODS, PERSONS

Introduction

Table 2 is the largest table in the DDC. It consists mainly of place names, which are sometimes very specific—e.g., Bryce Canyon National Park in Garfield County, Utah—and sometimes more general—e.g., Thailand. The more specific numbers tend to reflect the major English-speaking users of the classification scheme.

In addition to specific places, Table 2 provides for general geographic treatment by, for example, zone (e.g., tropics), type of vegetation (e.g., deserts), socioeconomic status (e.g., rural regions), and so on.

The historical periods listed in Table 1 are included in Table 2, so that they can be added in accordance with the instruction to "Add ... from Table 2". Similarly, -2 (Persons) is given here.

Geographic Treatment

A large number of subjects can be treated by place—e.g., football in the United States, Indian sculpture, cookery of Italy, and so on.

Some parts of the schedules include the place as an integral part of the classification number. For example,

190 Modern Western philosophy
191   United States and Canada
192   British Isles
and so on.

However, the geographic treatment of most subjects is represented by building a number using Table 2: Geographic areas, historical periods, persons (also called the Area table).

Table 2 (unlike Table 1) cannot be used without an instruction, e.g.,
Add to base number 759.9 notation 3-9 from Table 2, e.g., ...

The instruction always specifies the base number and the section of the table which you are entitled to use in this case.

Study the summary at the beginning of Table 2.
-1 deals with places not limited by continent, etc.—e.g., forests, oceans
-3 deals with the ancient world (although with the same overemphasis on European countries)
-4 to -9 cover the modern world, continent by continent. Within each continent, the notation divides into countries, then regions and so on

Area numbers can be found either by following the division of the larger place or by consulting the Relative Index.

Geography

The centered entry

> > 913-919 **Geography of and travel in ancient world and specific continents, countries, localities in modern world; extraterrestrial worlds**

carries the instruction

Add to base number 91 notation 3-9 from Table 2, ...

That is, write down the base number 91, then check Table 2 for the particular place. Note that this instruction restricts the notation to 3-9. That is, you can construct a number for the geography of any specific place in the ancient or modern world, but not the geography of places in general such as forests (-152).

For example,
Geography of Stone County (Mississippi)
Geography   91 +
Stone County (Mississippi)   -762 162   =   917.621 62

Geography of the Great Barrier Reef (Australia)
Geography   91 +
Great Barrier Reef   -943   =   919.43

Below the centered heading for 913-919, there is a table of other numbers to add, after you have made the geography number.

For example,
Travel in Stone County (Mississippi)
Geography of Stone County (Mississippi) 917.621 62 +
Travel   -04   =   917.621 620 4

An illustrated geography of the Great Barrier Reef (Australia)
Geography of the Great Barrier Reef   919.43 +
Illustrations   -00222   =   919.430 022 2

EXERCISE 8.1

Assign DDC numbers to the following:

1. The geography of Zimbabwe   _____

2. A textbook of the geography of Alaska   _____

3.   The Amazon River: a geography   _____

4.   Geography of ancient Rhodes   _____

5.   A guidebook for travel in the French Riviera   _____

6.   The travelers' guide to Spain   _____

7.   Prehistoric geography of Carthage   _____

8.   An illustrated guide to the geography of ancient England   _____

9.   A gazetteer of Southern Africa   _____

10. Bahrain: travel in the twentieth century   _____

History

The centered entry

> **930-990 History of ancient world; of specific continents, countries, localities; of extraterrestrial worlds**

carries the instruction

Add to base number 9 notation 3-9 from Table 2, ...

That is, write down the base number 9, then check Table 2 for the particular place. Note that again this instruction restricts the notation to 3-9. That is, you can construct a number for the history of any specific place in the ancient or modern world, but not the history of places in general such as forests (-152).

For example,
    History of Indonesia
    History   9 +
    Indonesia   -598   =   959.8

    History of Namibia
    History   9 +
    Namibia   -6881   =   968.81

Remember that when you have added the table number to the base number, always put the decimal point after the third digit.

Periods of History

Each country has its own period table, which must be used rather than the one in Table 1. These period tables apply to the country as a whole and to its subdivisions, such as states, provinces, cities, etc.

For example,

    History of Indonesia under the Dutch

History	9 +		
Indonesia	-598	=	959.8

    Now check the schedules at 959.8:

Dutch period, 1602-1945	=	959.802

    History of Namibia in the twentieth century

History	9 +		
Namibia	-6881	=	968.81

    Now check the schedules at 968.81:

South African period, 1915-1990	=	968.810 3

EXERCISE 8.2

Assign DDC numbers to the following:

1. A history of ancient Sparta   _____

2. A short history of the mountain regions of Bolivia   _____

3. The causes of World War II   _____

4. The United States under Ronald Reagan   _____

5. A history of the Thirty Years War   _____

6. The French Revolution   _____

7. The Russian Revolution   _____

8. History of the Persian Empire   _____

9. Norway in the 1950s: an outline history   _____

10. The encyclopedia of Zambian history   _____

Other Subjects

Many other subjects have instructions for adding from Table 2 to include geographic treatment in the complete classification number.

For example,

  372.9 Historical, geographic, persons treatment of elementary education
  carries the instruction "Add to base number 372.9 notation 01-9 from Table 2, ..."

  Elementary education in Brazil
  Base number   372.9 +
  Brazil   -81   =   372.981

EXERCISE 8.3

Assign DDC numbers to the following subjects:

1. Geology of Quebec   _____

2. Printmaking in Japan   _____

3. General statistics of Hungary   _____

4. Political conditions in the Irish Republic   _____

5. Economic conditions in Algeria   _____

6. Higher education in Vietnam   _____

7. Libraries in New Zealand   _____

8. The Roman Catholic Church in Paraguay _____

9. Constitutional law of ancient China   _____

10. Life expectancy in Burundi   _____

Adding from Table 2 without Instructions

There are many subjects in the schedules which may need geographical treatment, but which have no special instructions to add from Table 2.

However, special instructions are not needed to add from Table 1. So first add -09 from Table 1, then the area notation from Table 2.

For example,
  Boxing in Mexico
  Boxing   796.83 +
  Add -09 from Table 1   -09
  Mexico   -72 = 796.830 972

EXERCISE 8.4

Assign DDC numbers to the following:

1.   Snowmobiling in Scotland _____

2.   New Orleans brass bands _____

3.   Design and construction of buildings in Nagasaki _____

4.   Working mothers in ancient Rome _____

5.   Family counseling in Sweden _____

EXERCISE 8.5

Look at the schedules and Tables 1 and 2. Find the subject for each of the following numbers and supply a suitable title.

For example,
324.249 650 75 — The Communist Party of Albania

1.   942.052 007 2 _____

2.   954.035 005 _____

3.   306.743 094 93 _____

4.   283.753 _____

5.   372.959 3 _____

6.   996.11 _____

7.   359.009 611 _____

8.   759.949 2 _____

9.   026.340 257 663 8 _____

10. 974.710 430 92 _____

EXERCISE 8.6

Assign DDC numbers to the following. They include numbers direct from the schedules and numbers built by using Tables 1 and 2.

1.   Raising pigs   _____

2.   How to make soft toys   _____

3.   Surfacing dirt roads   _____

4.   Mobility of labor   _____

5.   Food and shelter for the needy   _____

6.   The encyclopedia of household pets   _____

7.   Teaching drawing   _____

8.   The theory of underwater photography   _____

9.   The philosophy of evolution   _____

10. Correspondence course in mathematics   _____

11. Radio in the 1930s   _____

12. The sociology of slavery in the Roman Empire   _____

13. Death customs in ancient Britain   _____

14. Theater in Zimbabwe   _____

15. Air pollution controls in Mexico   _____

16. Political parties in Peru   _____

17. Alligators of the Everglades   _____

18. Gold mining in Nevada   _____

19. Firefighting in Quebec Province   _____

20. Firefighting in the Gatineau Park (Quebec)   _____

EXERCISE 8.7

Assign DDC numbers to the following. They include numbers direct from the schedules and numbers built by using Tables 1 and 2.

1.   Modern archeology: techniques and equipment _____

2.   The dictionary of place names _____

3.   Maps of Irian Jaya _____

4.   Connecticut during the Colonial period _____

5.   Scotland in the 1960s _____

6.   Ohio history quarterly _____

7.   The diplomatic history of World War II _____

8.   Exploration of the moon _____

9.   Lake fishing _____

10.   Marine transportation across the Atlantic Ocean _____

11.   Baboons of the grasslands _____

12.   Wind systems in valleys _____

13.   Paintings in the seventeenth century _____

14.   Ancient Egypt during the Middle Kingdom _____

15.   The Thai Historical Association journal _____

16.   Life expectancy in Spain _____

17.   Modern British philosophy _____

18.   Customs of Easter Island _____

19.   Dictionary of building _____

20.   Experimental research in pharmaceutical chemistry _____

Chapter 9
TABLE 3: SUBDIVISIONS FOR THE ARTS, FOR INDIVIDUAL LITERATURES, FOR SPECIFIC LITERARY FORMS

Introduction

Table 3 is used with numbers from the 800 class (Literature and rhetoric). (Rhetoric is the branch of knowledge that treats the rules or principles of effective composition, whether in prose or verse; the art which teaches oratory.)

The 800s are used for works of the imagination; works of information should be classed with the subject.

Literature is restricted to:
- works of the imagination that are written in a particular form, e.g., poetry, fiction, drama
- criticism or description of such works
- history of a form (literary history) and biographies.

There are 3 sub-tables:

Table 3A	works by or about individual authors
Table 3B	works by or about more than one author
Table 3C	only used when an extra aspect of the work needs to be added.

Language

Literature is first treated according to the language in which it was originally written. The 800s are divided into:

800-809	Literature and rhetoric (in general)
810-819	American literature in English
820-829	English and Old English ... literatures
830-839	Literatures of Germanic ... languages
840-849	Literatures of Romance languages French literature
850-859	Literatures of Italian, ... Romanian, ... languages Italian literature
860-869	Literatures of Spanish and Portuguese languages
870-879	Literatures of Italic languages Latin
880-889	Literatures of Hellenic languages Classical Greek literature
890-899	Literatures of other specific languages and language families

Clearly this overemphasis on certain European literatures reflects the bias of American scholarship in Melvil Dewey's time. The allocation of so many literatures into 890-899 results in some very long numbers. There is also bias in favor of the "mother country" of the language, so that American and British literatures are well provided for, but Canadian, Australian, New Zealand, Indian, West Indian, and South African literatures in English are not.

This fault cannot be rectified without restructuring the 800s. Options are provided in an attempt to accommodate particular needs. For Canadian literature in English, options include:
- using 810-818 for American literature and 819 for Canadian literature in English
- classifying Canadian literature in English with American literature in 810-818
- using C810-C818 for Canadian literature in English
- classifying Canadian literature in English with English literature in 820-828.

There are also separate period tables for Canadian literature in English.

A similar set of options is available for Canadian literature in French, the literature of American countries in Spanish or Portuguese, and for other literatures requiring local emphasis.

Since practice varies, you should familiarize yourself with the policy and usage of one library you know well.

Form
The literary form of the work is considered next. Forms in Table 3 include:
- -1 Poetry
- -2 Drama
- -3 Fiction
- -4 Essays
- -5 Speeches
- -6 Letters
- -7 Humor and satire
- -8 Miscellaneous writings.

Some of these forms are further subdivided—e.g., Romantic fiction is a subdivision of Fiction. There is a preference table to look up when works have more than one form—e.g., a play in verse.

Period
Each major literature is further divided into recognized time periods, which are listed in the schedules at the number for the individual literature.

Other Aspects
It is also possible to reflect in the DDC number a particular aspect of a group of works. Classification numbers can represent works on a theme (e.g., Christmas), by particular people (e.g., children), or with a special feature (e.g., an experimental approach).

Literary Criticism
Literary criticism is classed with the literature being criticized. So discussion or criticism of a work is at the same number as the work itself (except optionally for Shakespeare and other very prolific authors). Criticism of several literatures is classed in 809.

Adaptations

An adaptation alters the form of a work or modifies its content in language, scope, or level of presentation so that it can no longer be considered a version of the original. It should then be classed as a work in its own right.

How to Add from Table 3

First decide whether the work is by one author or more than one author.

Table 3A: Works by or about One Author

1. Determine the original language. (This includes translations, which are classed with the original language.)
   Use the schedules (810-890) to find the *base number* for the language
       e.g., English   82

   Note that numbers from Table 3 can only be added to a base number, which is identified by the words "base number" or an asterisk (*). If a literature is not identified as a base number, do not add from Table 3. For example,
       Navaho poetry   897.2

2. If there is a specific literary form:
   Use Table 3A to find the number for the form
       e.g., poetry   -1
   Add it to the base number
       e.g., English poetry   82 + 1   =   821

   If there is no specific literary form:
   Go to the instructions under -8 in Table 3A

3. If there is a specific period:
   Use the schedules (810-890) to find the period table
       e.g., English poetry of the Victorian period   821 + 8 = 821.8

   Note that there are optional period tables for other English-language literatures
       e.g., for Canada, Australia, and so on.

EXERCISE 9.1

Find the base number for the following literatures:

   1. American (in English)   _____

   2. Dutch   _____

   3. Swedish   _____

   4. French   _____

5. Italian   _____

6. Catalan   _____

7. Portuguese   _____

8. Classical Greek   _____

9. Urdu   _____

10. Assamese   _____

11. Breton   _____

12. Slovak   _____

13. Kota   _____

14. Korean   _____

15. Xhosa   _____

EXERCISE 9.2

Find a DDC number for the following, using the schedules and Table 3A:

1. Poetry by an American poet   _____

2. A drama in Dutch by one author   _____

3. A collection of a Swedish novelist   _____

4. Short stories in English translation by a French author   _____

5. Letters written by a high-ranking Italian lady   _____

6. Speeches in Catalan by a famous politician   _____

7. A Portuguese author's miscellaneous writings   _____

8. Classical Greek poetry by a medieval poet   _____

9. Twentieth-century drama by an Urdu author   _____

10. A modern Assamese novel   _____

11. Letters by a sixteenth-century Breton   _____

12. Speeches by a Slovenian citizen in 1920-1930 _____

13. Poems of a Kota woman _____

14. Reminiscences of a Korean during the Yi period _____

15. Xhosa fiction _____

Table 3B: Works by or about More Than One Author

1. Determine the original language. (This includes translations, which are classed with the original language.)
   Use the schedules to find the base number for the language
   e.g., Chinese   895.1

2. If there is a specific literary form:
   Use Table 3B to find the number for the form
   e.g., drama   -2
   Add it to the base number
   e.g., Chinese drama   895.1 + 2   =   895.12

   If there is no specific literary form:
   Go to the instructions under -01-09 in Table 3B

3. If the literary form can be specified further (e.g., tragedy):
   Use Table 3B to find the more specific form
   e.g., tragedy   -20512
   Add it to the base number
   e.g., Chinese tragedy   895.1 + 20512   =   895.120 512

   If the literary form cannot be specified further, and if there is a specific period, go to step 4

4. If there is a specific period:
   Use the schedules to find the period table
   e.g., Chinese drama of the Ming dynasty
        895.12   +   46   =   895.124 6

EXERCISE 9.3

Find a DDC number for the following, using the schedules and Table 3A or 3B. Decide first whether the work is by one or more than one author:

1. The Penguin book of Chinese verse _____

2. Fifteenth-century English drama _____

3. French essays between the wars   _____

4. A yearbook of Finnish literature   _____

5. Essays of Umberto Eco translated from the Italian (late twentieth century)   _____

6. War and peace, a novel by Leo Tolstoy, translated from the Russian   _____

7. Mother Courage and her children, by Berthold Brecht, a tragedy translated from German, written 1936-1939   _____

8. Letters home: letters of Sylvia Plath, U.S. poet, late twentieth century   _____

9. Famous Greek ballads of the nineteenth century   _____

10. The Spanish love story   _____

Complex Numbers for Literature

It is possible to build extremely complex DDC numbers for literary works, e.g.,

An anthology of English limericks about cats	821.075 083 629 752
American television plays about death	812.025 083 548

However, for many libraries, this level of close classification is not appropriate. Libraries need to consider how many works they will have on these subjects and weigh the advantages of specificity against the disadvantages of very long numbers—on spines, on OPAC screens, for users to write down, for library staff to shelve, and so on.

Many libraries have policies about how specific their literature numbers are. For example, a library may decide that in the literature of a single language, only the form and time period will be reflected. Remember that classification is for the purpose of shelving like works together and helping users to find the material they want. Extremely long numbers are likely to be useful only in very large literature collections, where users are interested in very specific aspects of the literary works.

Complex Number-Building: Tables 3B and 3C

For full use of Table 3B, read and follow the instructions given at the beginning of the table. There is also a detailed explanation, including flowcharts, in the Manual entry on Table 3.

Many sections of Table 3B refer to another section, where instructions are to be followed. Be especially careful whether they refer to -1-8 or -102-108.

Remember only to add to any DDC number when there are instructions to add (other than standard subdivisions).

Table 3C: To Be Added Where Instructed

Table 3C enables many aspects of a literary work to be classified, including specific qualities of style (e.g., post-modernism), themes (e.g., seasons), subjects (e.g., religion), persons (e.g., for and by children, Vietnamese).

This table can also be used with some base numbers in the 700s. For example,

Urban themes in the arts   700.421 732
- 700.4   Special qualities of the arts (schedules—base number)
- 2   places (number following -3 in -32 in Table 3C)
- 1732   urban regions (Table 2)

Films portraying the Bible   791.436 822
- 791.436   Special aspects of films (schedules—base number)
- 82   Religious themes (number following -3 in -382 in Table 3C)
- 2   Bible (number following 2 in 220 Bible)

EXERCISE 9.4

Follow each step of the construction of the following numbers. You do not need to construct the numbers yourself.

Example: Collections of contemporary English-language poetry about Lincolnshire
821.914 080 324 253

- 82   English language literature (schedules—base number)
- 1   poetry (Table 3B)
- 914   later 20th century (schedules—English period table)
- 0   (as instructed at -11-19 in Table 3B)
- 80   collections (Table 3B)
- 32   about places (Table 3C)
- 4253   Lincolnshire (Table 2)

1. A collection of poetry for children   821.008 092 82

2. An anthology of American poetry about animals   811.008 036 2

3.   Poems by English women, Elizabethan to Victorian   821.008 092 87

4.   An anthology of modern American plays   812.540 8

5.   The Faber book of contemporary Latin American short stories   863.010 886 8

6.   Best sellers by French teenagers   843.009 928 3

7.   A critical study of Manx literature   891.640 9

| 8. | Soviet literature of the 1980s: a decade of transition | 891.709 004 4 |

| 9. | The Virago book of ghost stories | 823.087 33 |

| 10. | The journal of Beatrix Potter from 1881-1897 | 828.803 |

| 11. | The grotesque in the arts | 700.415 |

| 12. | Comedy films | 791.436 17 |

Chapter 10
TABLE 4: SUBDIVISIONS OF INDIVIDUAL LANGUAGES
AND
TABLE 6: LANGUAGES

Introduction

Table 4 is used with numbers from the 400 class (Language). Comprehensive works about both language and literature are classed in the 400s.

Table 6 is used with numbers from the schedules and other tables, whenever there is an instruction to add from Table 6.

Numbers from these tables are never used alone, and they are only used at all when there is an instruction to add from the appropriate table.

The Language Class

Like the 800s, the first part of 400 is concerned with the treatment of the subject in general. 410-419 (Linguistics) is the science and structure of spoken and written language.

Specific languages are located in 420-490. The 400s are divided into:

400-409	Standard subdivisions and bilingualism
410-419	Linguistics
420-429	English and Old English (Anglo-Saxon)
430-439	Germanic (Teutonic) languages German
440-449	Romance languages French
450-459	Italian, ..., Romanian, Rhaeto-Romanic languages
460-469	Spanish and Portuguese languages
470-479	Italic languages Latin
480-489	Hellenic languages Classical Greek
490-499	Other languages

The divisions of the 400 class follow the same pattern as the 800s. There is the same over-emphasis on European languages, so that non-European languages are squeezed into one division. This results in an uneven distribution of numbers through the class and much longer numbers for non-European language works.

There are options to give local emphasis to a specific language. These options are not used as frequently as the options for literature. Each library has its own policy about the use of options, depending on the type of collection and the needs of its users.

Table 4

Table 4 is divided into

-01-09	Standard subdivisions
-1	Writing systems, phonology, phonetics (standard)
-2	Etymology (standard)
-3	Dictionaries (standard)
-5	Grammar (standard)
-7	Historical and geographical variations, modern nongeographical variations (dialects, slang, etc.)
-8	Standard usage of the language

Note

- Do not use standard subdivisions -03 for dictionaries. They are an important part of language and have their own Table 4 number (-3).
- Phonology and phonetics deal with the sounds of a particular language.
- Etymology is concerned with the origin and history of a word.

How to Add from Table 4

1. Determine the language. Use the schedules (420-490) to find the *base number* for the language

     e.g., English   42

Note that numbers from Table 4 can only be added to a base number, which is identified by the words "base number" or an asterisk (*). If a language is not identified as a base number, do not add from Table 4. For example,

     A dictionary of Middle English   =   427.02

2. If there is a specific aspect of the language:
Use Table 4 to find the number

     e.g., grammar   -5

Add it to the base number

     e.g., English grammar   42 + 5   =   425

Examples

A Hungarian dictionary		494.511 3
494.511	Hungarian language (schedules - base number)	
3	dictionary (Table 4)	

History of the Korean language		495.709
495.7	Korean language (schedules - base number)	
09	history (Table 4 to Table 1 - standard subdivision)	

EXERCISE 10.1

Check the following numbers. Find the correct number if necessary.

1.	Mind your spelling (how to spell English words)	428.1
2.	Let's learn our ABCs	421.1
3.	A Chinese reader	495.1
4.	Street French: slang, idioms, and popular expletives (a historical approach)	447.09
5.	A crossword dictionary	423

EXERCISE 10.2

Assign DDC numbers for the following, using the schedules and Table 4.

1.	The Russian alphabet	_____
2.	The history of Hebrew	_____
3.	A new Lao reader	_____
4.	Spanish pronunciation	_____
5.	Modern German slang	_____
6.	A handbook of Malay script	_____
7.	Speak standard Indonesian	_____
8.	Teach yourself Swahili	_____
9.	English Creoles of the Caribbean	_____
10.	Portuguese as spoken in Brazil	_____

How to Add from Table 6

Table 6 provides numbers to add whenever instructed in the schedules or other tables. This enables language to be added as an aspect of many subjects, and a second language to be added to many numbers in the 400s (e.g., a bilingual dictionary).

The numbers do not necessarily correspond to the numbers in 420-490, although the pattern is very similar. Table 6 contains:

-1 Indo-European languages
-2 English and Old English (Anglo-Saxon)
-3 Germanic (Teutonic) languages
-4 Romance languages
-5 Italian, Sardinian, Dalmatian, Romanian, Rhaeto-Romanic
-6 Spanish and Portuguese languages
-7 Italic languages
-8 Hellenic languages
-9 Other languages

Follow the instructions to add from Table 6 whenever they occur, provided this level of specificity is appropriate for your library collection and users.

Examples

A Hungarian-English dictionary		494.511 321
494.511	Hungarian language (schedules - base number)	
3	dictionary (Table 4 -32-39)	
21	English (Table 6)	

The Bible in the Korean language		220.595 7
220.5	The Bible (schedules - base number)	
957	Korean language (Table 6)	

EXERCISE 10.3

Check the following numbers. Find the correct number if necessary.

1.	A quick beginners' course in Hindi for English speakers	491.438 342 1
2.	Speak Greek in a week (for English-speaking persons)	489.834 21
3.	Arabic phrase book (for English-speaking persons)	492.783
4.	Fluent English for Danish speakers	428.340 398 1
5.	A Dutch-English dictionary (one-way—i.e., with entries in Dutch only)	423.393 1
6.	A Japanese-German/German-Japanese dictionary	495.631

Bilingual Dictionaries

Read carefully the instruction in Table 4 at -32-39. A distinction is made between one-way dictionaries (i.e., with entry words in only one language) and two-way dictionaries (i.e., with entry words in both languages).

EXERCISE 10.4

Assign DDC numbers for the following, using the schedules and Tables 4 and 6:

1.   A French-Vietnamese dictionary   _____

2.   A Khmer-English/English-Khmer dictionary   _____

3.   Spanish words in the English language   _____

4.   Serial publications in Tagalog   _____

5.   Folktales in Yiddish   _____

Chapter 11
TABLE 5: RACIAL, ETHNIC, NATIONAL GROUPS
AND
TABLE 7: GROUPS OF PERSONS

Introduction
Tables 5 and 7 are both used to represent groups of people. Table 5 lists notation for racial, ethnic, and national groups, and Table 7 covers occupations and other characteristics (e.g., age, gender).

Both tables are used according to instructions which occur throughout the schedules and the other tables.

Table 5
Table 5 lists persons according to their racial, ethnic, and national origins. Numbers can be added either directly via an instruction, or indirectly by first adding -089 from Table 1 (which does not need a specific instruction). This enables the classifier to build a number for any subject studied by or in relation to any racial, ethnic or national group.

Table 5 includes:
-03-04	Basic races, mixtures of basic races
-1	North Americans
-2	British, English, Anglo-Saxons
-3	Nordic (Germanic) people
-4	Modern Latin peoples
-5	Italians, Romanians, related groups
-6	Spanish and Portuguese
-7	Other Italic peoples
-8	Greeks and related groups
-9	Other racial, ethnic, national groups.

Although the same European emphasis occurs in this table, it does assist the classifier to remember and locate particular numbers which appear in the schedules and several of the tables (e.g., Spanish contains -6 in the 400s, 800s, and Tables 2, 5, and 6).

Preference Order
Read the introduction to Table 5, which gives clear instructions as to which aspect to choose if there is more than one in the work. In summary, it is:
1. ethnic group
2. nationality
3. basic races.

How to Add from Table 5

With Specific Instructions
1. Identify the base number
     e.g., the sociology of social groups 305.8

2. Add from Table 5
     e.g., the sociology of the Inuit
          305.8   +   -9712   =   305.897 12

Without Specific Instructions
1. Identify the classification number
     e.g., athletic and outdoor sports and games   796

2. Check the number in the schedules for any specific instructions about standard subdivisions
     796.01-.09 Standard subdivisions

3. Add -089 from Table 1
     e.g., sports and games with respect to racial, ethnic, national groups
          796   +   -089   =   796.089

4. Add from Table 5
     e.g., Inuit sportspeople
          796.089   +   -9712   =   796.089 971 2

EXERCISE 11.1

Assign DDC numbers to the following subjects, using the schedules and Tables 1 and 5.

1.   Social anthropology of the Kurdish people   _____

2.   Social anthropology of French-Canadians   _____

3.   Bedouin art   _____

4.   Afrikaner folk music   _____

5.   Social services to Catalans   _____

6.   Metal engraving of Portuguese-speaking people   _____

7.   Child-rearing practices of the ancient Romans   _____

8.   Polynesian football players   _____

9.   Rum distilled by South American native people   _____

10.   Palestinian Christians   _____

Table 7

Table 7 lists persons according to occupations and other characteristics. As with Table 5, numbers can be added either directly via an instruction, or indirectly by first adding a standard subdivision from Table 1, particularly -024 or -088.

Table 7 includes:

-01-09	Nonoccupational characteristics
-1	Persons occupied with philosophy, parapsychology & occultism, psychology
-2	Persons occupied with or adherent to religion
-3	Persons occupied with social sciences & socioeconomic activity
-4	Persons occupied with languages, linguistics, lexicography
-5	Persons occupied with natural sciences & mathematics
-6	Persons occupied with applied sciences
-7	Persons occupied with the arts
-8	Persons occupied with creative writing & speaking
-9	Persons occupied with geography, history, etc.

There is a clear parallel with the classes 100-900, which helps in finding the relevant number in this table. The table must still be checked for the precise number and scanned for any relevant notes or other advice or instructions.

How to Add from Table 7

With Specific Instructions

1. Identify the base number
   e.g., occupational ethics   174.9

2. Add from Table 7
   e.g., the ethics of bankers
   174.9   +   -332   =   174.933 2

Without Specific Instructions

1. Identify the classification number
   e.g., geometry   516

2. Check the number in the schedules for any specific instructions about standard subdivisions
   516.001-.009   Standard subdivisions

3. Add -024 from Table 1
   e.g., geometry for persons in specific occupations
   516   +   -0024   =   516.002 4

4. Add from Table 7
   e.g., geometry for builders
   516.0024   +   -69   =   516.002 469

EXERCISE 11.2

Assign DDC numbers to the following, using the schedules and tables as required.

1.   Chemistry for potters   _____

2.   The ethics of psychologists   _____

3.   Preschool children as artists   _____

4.   The art of North American native peoples   _____

5.   Aerodynamics for ornithologists   _____

6.   Choreography for opera singers   _____

7.   An anthology of poetry by well-known detectives   _____

8.   Lesbian TV stars   _____

9.   Eritrean cooking in Los Angeles   _____

10. Civil and political rights in Muslim countries   _____

Chapter 12
ADDING FROM THE SCHEDULES

Introduction
Very specific numbers can be built using the auxiliary tables. DDC numbers can also be built by adding to a schedule number from elsewhere in the schedules.

Within the schedules there are many tables, which are enumerated for one subject but apply equally to other subjects of the same type. For example, the specific topics of animals, such as behavior, genetics, and so on, apply to each individual species of animal. Extra numbers are therefore listed once in the schedules, with instructions to copy this pattern for all the specific animal numbers.

There are also many numbers in the schedules, parts of which can be used with other numbers.

As with other number-building, you must follow the instructions and check the schedules when you have constructed the number to ensure that it does not conflict with another number.

Adding from the Schedules
Look at the following examples from the 900s:

987.063005		a journal of twentieth-century Venezuelan history
987		Venezuelan history
.063		20th century
	005	serial publication (standard subdivision, added by following the instruction "*Add as instructed under 930-990". Here we have a table of numbers to add to any of the numbers in the range 930-999—hence 005)

919.9104		exploration of the moon
919.91		geography of the moon
	04	exploration, travel (added by following the instruction "*Add as instructed under 913-919". Here we have a table of numbers to add to any of the numbers in the range 913-919—hence 04)

There are a number of ways to add from another part of the schedules.

Add a Direct Number from Another Part of the Schedules
Example: Agricultural libraries

1.   Identify the base number
   e.g., libraries 026
2.   Add notation 001-999 (i.e., any number in the schedules)
   e.g., agricultural libraries
      026 + 630 = 026.63

Add Part of a Number
Example: Secondary education for social responsibility

1.   Identify the base number
   e.g., 373.011 secondary education for specific objectives

2.   Add the numbers following 370.11 in 370.112-370.118 ...
   Look at the range 370.112-370.118 and find the number with the same aspect as we are looking for
   e.g., 370.115 education for social responsibility
   Write down the number 370.115
   The instruction states "numbers following 370.11"
   Draw a line after 370.11
   e.g., 370.11|5—this is the only number we want

   So, secondary education for social responsibility
      373.011 + 5 = 373.0115

Add from a Table in the Schedules
These tables can only be used when directed; the numbers to which they can be added are usually indicated by an asterisk (*) or a dagger (†).

1.   Identify the classification number
   e.g., racehorses 636.12*

2.   Follow instructions at the asterisk (*)
   e.g., *Add as instructed under 636.1-636.8

3.   Add from the table at 636.1-636.8
   e.g., Breeding racehorses
      636.12 + 2 = 636.122

EXERCISE 12.1

What do the following DDC numbers represent?

1. 940.316 2   _____

2. 025.171 6   _____

3. 255.530 09   _____

4. 725.210 87   _____

5. 782.107 941 _____

EXERCISE 12.2

Assign DDC numbers to the following, using the schedules and tables as required.

1. Financial journalists and journalism   _____

2. Snakes in the Bible   _____

3. Commerce in the Koran   _____

4. Conversion of non-Jews to Judaism in India   _____

5. Diseases in corn crops   _____

6. Restoration of commercial buildings   _____

7. Care of games in libraries   _____

8. Learning about crocodiles from museums   _____

9. Scientific works as literature   _____

10. Raising goats as stunt animals   _____

Chapter 13
DEWEY FOR WINDOWS

Introduction

Dewey for Windows (DFW) is an electronic version of the Dewey Decimal Classification, developed to maximize the usefulness of the scheme through the capacity to search electronically. In addition to the classification scheme contained in the four printed volumes, it provides a number of different approaches to searching.

Learning to Use *Dewey for Windows*

It is easier to use *Dewey for Windows* if you already have an overall grasp of the scheme, especially the hierarchy and the procedure for building numbers. If you are new to DDC, refer to earlier chapters of this book to gain an understanding of the structure before you begin to use *Dewey for Windows*.

Dewey for Windows offers an interactive tutorial, "TourGuide", which is recommended for all users. It demonstrates the tools, techniques, and structure of the package, and shows how to find DDC numbers using *Dewey for Windows*. The program assumes a working knowledge of the Windows interface. Users who are not familiar with Windows are advised to do the Windows tutorial before they begin.

Views

Using the printed DDC often requires you to have more than one volume open at once. You may begin with a summary (Volume 2), then consult the Relative Index (Volume 4), then look for a number in a table (Volume 1) and check the schedules (Volume 2 or 3) at the same time.

Dewey for Windows enables you to see different parts of the scheme together by providing a variety of "Views". There are four standard views—Browse, Search, Scan, and Summary—plus the capacity for you to create your own views if you wish. You will need to work with *Dewey for Windows* for a while before you become familiar with the advantages and disadvantages of different approaches, and identify the view/s best suited to your particular style. You can compare views by switching between them during a search.

The standard views are each described in the *Dewey for Windows* Reference Card. Read the descriptions and tips, and think about the way you currently use DDC. For instance,
- How extensively do you use the first, second, and third summaries to locate a likely place for the work you are classifying?
- How heavily do you rely on the Relative Index?
- Do you begin a search by reviewing the hierarchy from the broadest to the most specific numbers, or do you start with the Relative Index, and just use the hierarchy to check that your number is in the right place?

As classifiers use the printed DDC in different ways, so there are different ways to use *Dewey for Windows*. When you begin, you may rely heavily on the DDC Pages window, since this most closely resembles the printed work.

The following exercises are designed to introduce you to using the standard views. Become familiar with these and with simple searches, and then try following the instructions in the DFW Reference Card to focus and/or expand your searches. Over time you will establish your preferred approaches; you may settle on using one standard view, choose different views for different searches (e.g., checking a number derived by someone else vs. creating your own number), or make your own view or views.

In any view, you can:
- maximize any window to see a larger display
- choose Display to see appropriate Library of Congress Subject Headings
- choose Bib Rec. to see a sample record using the number selected
- choose LCSH to review the frequency of headings used with the number
- choose Print to print the contents of the active window
- choose Notes to make a permanent record of a DDC number and its specific use
- choose Past to review the searches you have made during the current session
- use Help to understand a term or procedure.

EXERCISE 13.1

Assign DDC numbers to the following subjects and titles, beginning with the Browse View.

Example

Manufacturing outdoor furniture
1. In the Search For input box, enter "outdoor furniture"; click Search
2. The terms displayed are:

392.36	Dwelling places
645.8	Outdoor furnishings
648.5	Housecleaning
684.12-684.16	Specific kinds of furniture
684.18	Outdoor furniture
749.3	Specific kinds of furniture
749.8	Outdoor furniture

3. Identify the likely numbers and check their hierarchy
4. Choose "684.18" Outdoor furniture for closer examination
5. Click Display to see notes, index and LCSH terms
6. Drag "684.18 Outdoor furniture" and drop it in the DDC Pages window to scan related information
7. Choose 684.18

1. A guide to coffee table design   _____

2. Growing begonias   _____

3.   The law of income tax   _____

4.   Aerial photography   _____

5.   Upholstering your sofa   _____

EXERCISE 13.2

Check the following DDC numbers, and correct them if necessary, beginning with the Browse View.

1.	The Crusades	909.07
2.	Radio advertising	659.1402
3.	The Apostles' Creed	238.11

EXERCISE 13.3

Assign DDC numbers to the following subjects, beginning with the Search View.

Example
Social change
1.   In the Search For input box, enter "social change"; click Search
2.   The terms displayed are:

M	004-006	(Data processing Computer science)
	004	Data processing Computer science
C	302-307	Specific topics in sociology & anthropology
	302.23	Media (Means of communication)
	303.4	Social change
M	303.48 vs. 306.4	Causes of change vs. Specific aspects of culture
	303.482	Contact between cultures
	303.483	Development of science & technology
M	303.483 vs. 306.45	Development of science & technology [as causes of social change]
	303.484	Purposefully induced change
	303.49	Social forecasts
	303.66	War
	306.34	Systems of production and exchange
	320.52	Conservatism
	371.81	Student movements

3.   In the 300s, note that there is a centered entry:

C	302-307	Specific topics in sociology & anthropology

and 2 Manual entries:

M	303.48 vs. 306.4	Causes of change vs. Specific aspects of culture
M	303.483 vs. 306.45	Development of science & technology [as causes of social change] vs. Science [and] Technology [as cultural institutions]

4.   Click Display (or double-click the entry) to see the discussion in the Manual
5.   Choose the number which best suits the emphasis in the work you are classifying

1. Causes of unemployment   _____

2. Schools of linguistics   _____

3. Modern British sheep breeds   _____

4. Modern art   _____

5. Church architecture   _____

EXERCISE 13.4

Assign DDC numbers to the following subjects, beginning with the Scan View.

Example
    Library classification
    1.   In the Scan For input box, enter "library classification".
    2.   Change "Basic index" to "Rel. Index (phrases)" to search the Relative Index of DDC. Click Scan, or press Return
    3.   There is no matching entry, though there are many entries beginning with "Library" and "Libraries" which you could scan
    4.   In the Scan For input box, change "library classification" to "classification". Click Scan, or press Return
    5.   The terms displayed include
          Classification—information science
    6.   Click Search (or double-click the entry) to see
          025.42   Classification and shelf listing
    7.   Click Display (or double-click the entry) to see the detail of this number, including notes and LC subject terms
    8.   Choose 025.42

1. Chemical contraception   _____

2. Educating children with communicative disorders   _____

3. Sports injuries   _____

4. Fashion modeling   _____

5. Bringing up children   _____

EXERCISE 13.5

Find the meaning of the following DDC numbers, beginning with the Summary View.

Example
What does 398.8 represent?
1. In the DDC Summary window, click on "300 Social sciences", and click Expand (or double-click "300 Social sciences")
2. Click on "390 Customs, etiquette, folklore", and click Expand (or double-click "390 Customs, etiquette, folklore")
3. Click on "398 Folklore", and click Expand (or double-click "398 Folklore")
4. Choose "398.8 Rhymes and rhyming games"
5. Drag "398.8 Rhymes and rhyming games" and drop it in the DDC Pages window to check the description

1. 496.398 5 _____

2. 551.642 53 _____

3. 077.31 _____

EXERCISE 13.6

Assign DDC numbers to the following subjects and titles, beginning with the Summary View.

1. Etruscan sculpture _____

2. Dinosaurs _____

3. Halley's comet _____

4. A history of drug addiction _____

5. Having twins: a parent's guide to pregnancy, birth and early childhood _____

Chapter 14
MORE PRACTICE

EXERCISE 14.1
What do the following DDC numbers represent?

1. 005.373 5 _____

2. 070.593 _____

3. 133.54 _____

4. 155.937 _____

5. 268.67 _____

6. 303.484 _____

7. 920.72 _____

8. 590.734 6 _____

9. 428.42 _____

10. 423.1 _____

11. 509.2 _____

12. 428.405 _____

13. 658.45 _____

14. 786.509 2 _____

15. 796.323 082 _____

EXERCISE 14.2

Assign DDC numbers to the following works.

1. Thailand: description and travel

    _____

2. Wisconsin: discovery and exploration (1795-1869)

    _____

3. Vancouver Island (B.C.): description and travel in the nineteenth century

    _____

4. Asia: description and travel in the 1980s

    _____

5. The waterfalls of Hawaii: a description

    _____

6. Natural monuments in Central America: a pictorial work

    _____

7. The Rand McNally guide to the coasts of Massachusetts, New Hampshire and Maine (a work designed to show points of interest in the 1980s)

    _____

8. A guidebook for travel in Colorado

    _____

9. An illustrated guide to the geography of ancient England

    _____

10. Geographic features of ancient Rhodes

    _____

11. Travel in India during 318-500 A.D.

    _____

12. The cities of ancient Egypt: a geography

    _____

13. Prehistoric geography of Carthage

    _____

14. Maps of Yellowstone National Park

    _____

15. Atlas of the ancient world

    _____

EXERCISE 14.3

Assign DDC numbers to the following works.

1. Atlas of the oceans of the world

    _____

2. Physical geography of mountains

    _____

3. An illustrated atlas of islands

    _____

4. Maps of the Mediterranean Sea in the eighteenth century

    _____

5. Maps of the ancient Roman Empire

    _____

6. Spiritualism in Catholic countries

    _____

7. Trade unions in Argentina

    _____

8. Social welfare services to the mentally ill in British Columbia

    _____

9. A guide to the snakes of Ireland

    _____

10. Rail passenger transport in Belgium

    _____

11. Printmaking in France

    _____

12. Waterbirds of the world

    _____

13. Local government in the Southern Hemisphere

    _____

14. Birds of the Indian Ocean

    _____

15. A guide to wine making in Virginia

    _____

EXERCISE 14.4

Assign DDC numbers to the following works.

1. Transplants in Transylvania

    _____

2. The paintings of Tom Thomson (Canadian)

    _____

3. Postage stamps of Angola

    _____

4. Country music from Texas

    _____

5. Horse racing tracks in Hong Kong

    _____

6. Horse riding in Wyoming

    _____

7. Hunting in South Africa in the nineteenth century

    _____

8. German Christian church architecture of the sixteenth century

    _____

9. *The Sydney Morning Herald* & other Sydney newspapers

    _____

10. Folksongs of Chile

    _____

11. Dutch narrative poetry

    _____

12. Spanish farce

    _____

13. Twentieth-century Spanish drama

    _____

14. The modern Indonesian novel—the works of Pramoedya Ananta Toer

    _____

15. An Indonesian dictionary

    _____

EXERCISE 14.5

Assign DDC numbers to the following works.

1. English-Indonesian dictionary

   _____

2. English-Indonesian-English dictionary

   _____

3. Dictionary of Indonesian acronyms

   _____

4. Use of French words in English

   _____

5. English for Spanish people

   _____

6. English for Malayalam-speaking people

   _____

7. Choral singing for the hearing impaired

   _____

8. Case histories in psychiatry

   _____

9. Pasteur the chemist: a biography

   _____

10. General biology: a quarterly magazine

    _____

11. A guide to fascist political theory

    _____

12. Harrap's Russian dictionary

    _____

13. The Roman Catholic Church in Spain

    _____

14. The journal of sports medicine

    _____

15. Kenya before the British

    _____

EXERCISE 14.6

Assign DDC numbers to the following works.

1.   How to read maps

                                                             _____

2.   Make-up for pantomime

  _____

3.   The ethics of euthanasia

  _____

4.   Biographies of ancient Egyptians

  _____

5.   Biographies of notable Jamaicans

  _____

6.   The movement for women's suffrage

  _____

7.   The Pankhursts: a biography

  _____

8.   Modern archeology: techniques and equipment

  _____

9.   Genealogical sources of Scotland

  _____

10.   An introduction to historiography

  _____

11.   The spiritual discipline of yoga

  _____

12.   Erotica in art

  _____

13.   Design of caravan parks for long-term residents

  _____

14.   An introduction to mechanical pumps

  _____

15.   Dictionary of biology

  _____

EXERCISE 14.7

Assign DDC numbers to the following works.

1. Dutch poetry of the seventeenth century

    _____

2. The design of motels for the aged

    _____

3. First aid for gunshot wounds

    _____

4. Scotland under James II

    _____

5. Modern joinery: a guide to North American practice

    _____

6. Preparing microscopic plant slides

    _____

7. Scale models of solar-powered automotive engines

    _____

8. Manufacture of toilet tissue: patents

    _____

9. Research in the manufacture of hand tools

    _____

10. Underwriting health and accident insurance

    _____

11. English fiction: a secondary school study guide

    _____

12. The Robben Island prison riot

    _____

13. The San Diego Museum of Art

    _____

14. The design of tugboats

    _____

15. A zoological study of clams, mussels and cuttlefish

    _____

EXERCISE 14.8

What do the following DDC numbers represent?

1. 549.911

2. 513.071 2

3. 634.709 777

4. 853.914

5. 912.431 55

6. 978.112 5

7. 025.065 786 809 759

8. 004.015 1

9. 285.295 95

10. 296.830 974 811

11. 305.488 958 073

12. 324.630 899 755

13. 338.274 309 959 2

14. 362.102 308 2

15. 378.33

EXERCISE 14.9

Assign DDC numbers to the following works.

1. Traditional Jewish rites: Bar mitzvah

   _____

2. Research into the manufacture of synthetic perfumes

   _____

3. Collecting pistols

   _____

4. The Kansas City Jazz Festival

   _____

5. How to lip-read

   _____

6. Corals of the Australian Barrier Reef

   _____

7. Canada under Trudeau

   _____

8. The building of rock-fill dams in the nineteenth century

   _____

9. Nursing aged psychiatric patients

   _____

10. Nebraska between the World Wars

    _____

11. Residential care for heroin addicts

    _____

12. Prostitution in the twentieth century: a sociological study

    _____

13. Photographs of animals

    _____

14. Rotary clubs in South Carolina

    _____

15. The mining of tin

    _____

Exercise 14.10

What do the following DDC numbers represent?

1. 181.07

    _____

2. 153.947 96

    _____

3. 155.911 67

    _____

4. 428.340 706 69

    _____

5. 331.124 100 5

    _____

6. 331.137 810 274

    _____

7. 331.119 66

    _____

8. 331.252 916 59

    _____

9. 331.413 7

    _____

10. 338.372 757

    _____

11. 336.266 73

    _____

12. 230.98

    _____

13. 220.52033

    _____

14. 230.071 185

    _____

15. 220.872 582 702 89

    _____

ANSWERS

EXERCISE 1.1
Our world is classified by an infinite number of schemes, from the organization of supermarket shelves to scientific classification of species and subspecies to the grouping and ranking of employees in the workplace, whether by qualifications, duties performed, salary and/or status and so on.

EXERCISE 1.2
Possible criteria for organizing your "zoo" include:
> geographic origin—e.g., all the African animals in one place
> habitat—e.g., all the tropical animals together
> species—e.g., all the birds together
> diet—e.g., all the carnivores together.

The point of the exercise is for you to see that there is more than one way of grouping objects (topics) together. Questions to consider include whether your scheme is able to accommodate all the animals and whether it provides a reasonably even distribution of animals. Once you have decided on your criteria, it is important to be consistent.

REVIEW QUIZ 1.3

1. The primary reason is to arrange items on the library shelves according to their subject content.
   Other reasons include:
   - bringing related items together in a helpful sequence;
   - providing formal orderly access to the shelves either through a direct search of the shelves (browsing) or via the catalog;
   - enabling easy reshelving of library materials; and
   - providing an order for the classified catalog.

2. Enumerative classification attempts to spell out (enumerate) all the single and composite subject concepts required:
   > e.g., Library of Congress Classification, Dewey Decimal Classification (to a lesser extent).
   Synthetic classification lists numbers for single concepts, and allows the classifier to construct (synthesize) numbers for composite subjects:
   > e.g., Colon Classification, Universal Decimal Classification, some features of DDC.

3. Classification schedules are arranged in number order. This enables the classifier to see the relationships between topics, and to find closely related numbers.

4. Number building is the construction of classification numbers not listed in the schedules, following rules given in the scheme. It allows for more specific numbers to be created, and saves a great deal of space in the schedules.

5. Hierarchical classification is classification in which the division of subjects is from the most general to the most specific. Each number is included in the number above it in the hierarchy, so that each subordinate subject is classified at a more specific number within the same hierarchy.

6.   Since the primary purpose of classification is to group works according to their subject content in order to facilitate their access and use, it is important to consider who are the users and what organization of material is most useful to them.

EXERCISE 2.1

615.954	361
616	361.003
616.091	361.02
616.11	361.04
616.122	361.1
616.123	361.103
616.1237	361.2
616.125	361.23
616.200475	361.3
616.2009	361.301
616.201	361.32
616.24	361.3205
616.240083	361.320994
616.241	361.322
616.244	361.323
617.0083	361.32305
617.08	361.37
617.44	361.37025
617.80083	361.3703

REVIEW QUIZ 2.2

1.   Dewey Decimal Classification is divided into ten main classes. These are each divided into ten divisions, each of which is divided into ten sections.

2.   The First, Second and Third Summaries list the main classes, divisions and sections with their headings. They are used to become familiar with the overall structure of DDC, and to locate numbers which relate to each other.

3.   The Relative Index relates topics to all of their aspects by showing all the numbers for a topic in the different disciplines to which they belong.

4.   The advantages of DDC include:
   • DDC was the first to use the concept of relative location to organize materials on the shelf.
   • The pure notation (i.e., all Arabic numbers) is recognized internationally.
   • The straightforward numerical sequence facilitates filing and shelving.
   • The Relative Index brings together different aspects of the same subject which are scattered in different disciplines.
   • The hierarchical notation expresses the relationship between and among class numbers.
   • The decimal system enables infinite expansion and subdivision.
   • The mnemonic notation helps users to memorize and recognize class numbers.
   • Periodic revision keeps it up-to-date.

5.   The disadvantages of DDC include:
   • Its Anglo-American bias is evident in its emphasis on American, English, and European language, literature, and history in the 400s, 800s, and 900s, and Protestantism/Christianity in the 200s.

- Some related disciplines are separated: e.g., 400 and 800, 300 and 900.
- Some subjects are not very comfortably placed:

  e.g.,   Library science in 000

  Psychology as part of Philosophy in 100

  Sports and amusements in 700.
- In the 800s, literary works by the same author are scattered according to form.
- Decimal numbering limits its capacity for accommodating subjects on the same level because there can only be 9 divisions (+ 1 general division).
- Different rates of growth of some disciplines have resulted in an uneven structure:

  e.g.,   300 and 600 are particularly overcrowded.
- Although theoretically expansion is infinite, it doesn't allow infinite insertion between related numbers:

  e.g.,   between 610 and 619.
- Specificity results in long numbers, which can be awkward for shelving and on spine labels.
- Altering numbers because of a new edition creates practical problems in libraries,

  e.g.,   the need for reclassification, relabeling, and reshelving.

EXERCISE 3.1

1.   Epilepsy—1, 2, 5
2.   Art—1, 2, 5, 9
3.   Astrology—1, 2, 5
4.   Whichever of fishing and boating comes first in DDC—1, 2, 7
5.   Social sciences—1, 2, 3
6.   Japanese fiction—1, 4
7.   This could be any one of a wide range of subjects, including psychology, philosophy, religion, and anatomy—1, 2, 5
8.   Geography of Seattle—1, 2, 5, 6
9.   World literature—1, 2, 4
10. Geography of Australia or Urban planning in Australia—1, 2, 9
11. Bible—1, 2, 5
12. Inflation, then Bolivia—1, 2, 5, 12
13. Whichever of apples and pears comes first in DDC—1, 2, 7
14. Apples—1, 2, 5
15. Fruit—1, 2, 5, 9
16. Stone fruit—1, 2, 5, 9
17. Berry fruit—1, 2, 14
18. Painting, then landscape painting, then Canada—1, 2, 5, 13
19. Composting, then North America—1, 2, 5, 16
20. Religion—1, 2, 5

EXERCISE 3.2

Subject	Classification Heading	Broad / Close
Family therapy	Family therapy	close
Marital relationship	Marriage & family	broad
Atlanta's history	History of Georgia	broad
Marriage counseling	Family problems & services	broad

Business mathematics	Mathematics	broad
Modern Spanish Bible	Modern language Bibles	broad
The Shakers (religious group)	Adherents of religious groups	broad
Blood	Blood	close
Banking in Mexico	Mexican banks & banking	close
Christian Church's views on sex, marriage & family	Christian attitudes on sex, marriage & family	broad/close, depending on whether you think the Church's attitudes equate to Christian attitudes

REVIEW QUIZ 3.3

1.   As much as is needed to be confident of what it is about.

2.   Since DDC is based on disciplines, you need to decide in which discipline the subject belongs.

3.   Broad classification uses the main divisions and subdivisions of a scheme without breaking down into narrower concepts.
Close classification means classifying each work as specifically as possible, using all available subdivisions in the classification scheme.
> e.g.,   for a work on growing apples in Tasmania,
> the number for fruit-growing is broad classification;
> apple-growing in Tasmania is close classification.

4.   Citation order is the order in which you are instructed to add different aspects of a subject.
Preference order is the order in which to choose one aspect when a subject has more than one aspect, but the rules allow only one to be added.
They are different, since citation order allows more than aspect to be reflected, whereas preference requires a choice to be made.

5.   A call number usually consists of a classification number, a book number and often a location symbol. It is the number on a library item which shows where it is located.

6.   • Stocktaking can be done by reading the barcodes on the items with a wand, and using the online catalog to compare this information with its database.
   • Classification numbers can be checked direct from the catalog.
   • Subject bibliographies can be produced from the catalog.
   • The catalog can be used for insurance purposes, as a record of the library's holdings.

EXERCISE 4.1

1.	My book of opera	700
2.	A child's Bible	200
3.	Three Irish plays	800
4.	World Book encyclopedia	000
5.	Teach yourself Vietnamese	400

6.	The psychology of violence	100
7.	Russian rockets	600
8.	Physics for beginners	500
9.	Road atlas of New Zealand	900
10.	Employment of aged persons	300
11.	Multicultural education	300
12.	Encyclopaedia of Papua New Guinea	900
13.	How to draw cartoons	700
14.	Introductory philosophy	100
15.	Agricultural pest control	600

EXERCISE 4.2

1.	Audiovisual materials in libraries		020
2.	Japanese printmaking		760
3.	Growing wheat for export		630
4.	Twentieth-century architecture		720
5.	A concise history of Chile		980
6.	The nursing handbook		610
7.	Paleontological studies		560
8.	Women into politics		320
9.	A historical atlas of ancient Egypt		910
10.	Carnivorous plants		580
11.	The Methodist Church in the Pacific		270
12.	Abortion	(ethics)	170
		or (medicine)	610
13.	The planet Mars		520
14.	How to play hockey		790
15.	Learn Polish: an audiovisual approach		490
16.	The Oxford English dictionary		420
17.	Caring for rare books		090
18.	Child psychology		150
19.	The legal handbook		340
20.	Jewish folktales		390

EXERCISE 4.3

1.	Developing educational curricula	375
2.	Harrap's new German grammar	435
3.	The plays of William Shakespeare	822
4.	Electricity	537
5.	Let's visit Kenya	916
6.	The philosophy of Socrates	183
7.	Southeast Asian cooking	641
8.	What bird is that?	598
9.	Journalism in the new Russia	077
10.	Steam trains for enthusiasts	625
11.	Islam	297
12.	Introduction to trout fishing	799

EXERCISE 4.4

1. 900 is superordinate to all the other numbers (930, 938, 938.03).
2. 930 is subordinate to 900.
3. 938.03 is subordinate to 938.

REVIEW QUIZ 4.5

1. Disciplines form the basic structure of DDC. In the DDC, subjects are arranged by disciplines.

2. Hierarchy is the arrangement of subjects and the numbers which represent them in a structure where more specific subjects are part of, and subordinate to, broader subjects. It is fundamental to DDC, since it allows the classifier to find specific numbers in their relationship with more general ones.

3. 155 is superordinate to 155.4. This means that 155 (Differential and developmental pyschology) includes 155.4 (Child pyschology), or that 155.4 (Child pyschology) is part of 155 (Differential and developmental pyschology).

4. It is likely to be a very specific number. Each number which is subordinate to another number is one digit longer. Therefore the more specific the subject, the longer the number.

5. The auxiliary tables enable more specific numbers to be made, by adding a particular aspect of a subject to a number from the schedules. For example, the number for an encyclopedia of folklore is constructed by adding -03 (dictionaries, encyclopedias, concordances) from Table 1 to 398 (Folklore) to give 398.03.

6. No. Although the index is very comprehensive, it does not include all the aspects of all possible subjects— e.g., American short stories, educational statistics.

7. It is called the Relative Index because it relates all the aspects of a subject which may belong in different classes—e.g.,
   Mothers
family relationships	306.874 3
guides to Christian life	248.843 1
psychology	155.646 3

8. The interdisciplinary number for helicopters is 387.733 52.

9. The Manual (in Volume 4) gives an explanation at *550 vs. 910*

10. The Glossary (in Volume 1) gives the definition: "The rule instructing that works that give equal treatment to three or more subjects that are all subdivisions of a broader subject are classified in the first higher number that includes all of them." For example, a work on growing coconuts, avocados and papayas is classified at the number for growing tropical and subtropical fruits.

EXERCISE 5.1

1. An illustrated history of 15th century Japan
Main subject:	History of Japan
Secondary aspect:	15th century
Secondary aspect:	illustrated

2. A dictionary of terms for motorists
                Main subject: Motoring
                Secondary aspect: dictionary

3. The history of glass-blowing in Venice in the Middle Ages
                Main subject: Glass-blowing
                Secondary aspect: history
                Secondary aspect: in Venice
                Secondary aspect: in the Middle Ages

EXERCISE 5.2

1. Class: 000   Specific term(s): KWIC indexing / KWOC indexing
    DDC number: 025.486

2. Class: 300   Specific term(s): Disposal of dead *see also* Undertaking (Mortuary)—law
    DDC number: 344.045

3. Class: 300   Specific term(s): Home care services
    DDC number: 362.14
    or
    Class: 600   Specific term(s): Home care services   362.14 *see also 649.8 for home care by family members*
    DDC number: 649.8
    or
    Class: 600   Specific term(s): Nursing
    DDC number: 610.734 3

4. Class: 100   Specific term(s): Homosexuality—ethics
    DDC number: 176
    or
    Class: 200   Specific term(s): Homosexuality—ethics—religion
    DDC number: 291.566 (comparative religion), 294.356 6 (Buddhism), 241.66 (Christianity), 294.548 66 (Hinduism), 296.366 (Judaism)

5. Class: 900   Specific term(s): Twelve Tribes
    DDC number: 933.02

6. Class: 600   Specific term(s): Adobe—building construction
    DDC number: 693.22
    or
    Class: 700   Specific term(s): Adobe—architectural construction
    DDC number: 721.044 22

7. Class: 300   Specific term(s): Blood banks
    DDC number: 362.178 4

8. Class: 200   Specific term(s): God—Islam
    DDC number: 297.211

9. Class: 500   Specific term(s): Volcanoes
    DDC number: 551.21

10. Class: 300   Specific term(s): Family counseling
     DDC number: 362.828 6

11. Class: 100   Specific term(s): Perception—psychology
     DDC number: 153.7
     or
     Class: 100   Specific term(s): Perception—psychology—sensory
     DDC number: 152.1
     see Manual at 153.7 vs. 152.1

12. Class: 100   Specific term(s): Philosophers—Oriental or Ancient philosophy
     DDC number: 181.11

13. Class: 300   Specific term(s): Hazardous materials—public safety
     363.17 *For hazardous materials as components of articles that become hazardous products, see 363.19*
     or
     Class: 300   Specific term(s): Toys—product safety
     DDC number: 363.19

14. Class: 700   Specific term(s): School buildings *see also Educational buildings.* Educational buildings—
     architecture
     DDC number: 727

15. Class: 900   Specific term(s): World War II
     DDC number: 940.531 1

EXERCISE 6.1

1. | 300 | Social sciences |
    | 340 | Law |
    | 345 | Criminal law |
    | 345.07 | Criminal trials |
    | 345.072 | Pretrial procedure (for criminal trials) |

2. | 600 | Technology (Applied sciences) |
    | 650 | Management and auxiliary services |
    | 659 | Advertising and public relations |
    | 659.1 | Advertising |
    | 659.14 | Advertising by broadcast media |
    | 659.143 | Television advertising |

3. | 300 | Social sciences |
    | 370 | Education |
    | 375 | (Educational) curricula |
    | 375.001 | Curriculum development |

4. | 500 | Natural sciences and mathematics |
    | 590 | Animals |
    | 599 | Mammals |
    | 599.9 | Hominidae   Homo sapiens |
    | 599.97 | Human races |
    | 599.972 | Origins and causes of physical differences among races |

5. 910   Geography and travel
    910.4   Accounts of travel
    910.45   Ocean travel and seafaring adventures
    910.452   (Accounts of) Shipwrecks

EXERCISE 6.2

There are hundreds (thousands?) of examples of each of these. One example of each is provided here—only check the answers given if you were unable to find an example, or are not sure whether you correctly understand the term.

1. A heading—700   The arts   Fine and decorative arts

2. A summary—see the First, Second and Third Summaries at the beginning of Volume 2

3. A centered heading— >180-190 Historical, geographic, persons treatment of philosophy

4. A subordinate number—394.6 Fairs is subordinate to 394 General customs

5. A relocated topic—[376] Education of women
                Relocated to 371.822

6. A class-elsewhere note—728.1 Low-cost housing
                Class specific types of low-cost housing in 728.3-728.7

7. A see-also reference—641.5636 Vegetarian cooking
                See also 641.65 for cooking vegetables

8. A see reference—741 Drawing and drawings
                For drawing and drawings by subject, see 743

9. A scope note—022 Administration of the physical plant (of libraries)
                Including reading rooms and other special rooms, bookmobiles

10. An option—810-890 Literature of specific languages
    Literature is classed by the language in which originally written
    (Option: Class translations into a language requiring local emphasis with the literature of that language)

EXERCISE 6.3

1. 621.3276   Sodium-vapor lighting
    621.324   Gas lighting
    628.95   Public lighting
    None of the numbers covers all aspects of the subject. The correct number could be 621.3276 (Sodium-vapor lighting) or 628.95 (Public lighting), depending on whether "sodium-vapor" or "public" was more important.

2. 788.94   Horns (musical instruments)
    681.8   Manufacture of musical instruments
    736.6   Carving ivory, bone, horn, shell, amber
    736.6 (Carving ivory, bone, horn, shell, amber) most closely classifies the subject.

3.   398.3   Natural and physical phenomena as subjects of folklore
     398.365   Minerals as subjects of folklore
     549.23   Metals (Mineralogy)
     739.22   Goldsmithing (Art metalwork)
     553.41   Formation and structure of gold deposits
     398.365 (Minerals as subjects of folklore) most closely classifies the subject.

4.   364.44   Welfare services in the prevention of crime and delinquency
     362.88   Problems of and services to victims of crime
     363.23   Police functions as part of Social problems and services; association
                  (Class here prevention of crime by police)
     365.46   (Penal and related) institutions for the criminally insane
     362.88 (Problems of and services to victims of crime) most closely classifies the subject (unless another aspect is particularly emphasized).

5.   665.5384   Technology of heavy fuel oil (including absorber oil, diesel fuel, gas oil, heating oil)
     621.4025   Equipment for heat engineering
     644.1   Heating (Household utilities)
     644.1 (Heating [Household utilities]) most closely classifies the subject.

6.   616.12   Diseases of the heart
     617.412   Heart surgery
     641.56311   Cooking for persons with heart disease
     614.5912   Incidence of and public measures to prevent heart disease
     614.5912 (Incidence of and public measures to prevent heart disease) most closely classifies the subject.

EXERCISE 6.4

1.   The history of the Punic Wars   937.04
2.   An introduction to photochemistry   541.35
3.   Big game hunting   799.26
4.   How valleys are formed   551.442
5.   The Ouija board in spiritualism   133.932 5
6.   The identification of waterbirds   598.176
7.   How to read maps   912.014
8.   The Lutheran Church in America   284.133
9.   New ideas in tax reform   336.205
10. Unemployment resulting from technological change   331.137 042
11. Cycle racing   796.62
12. Behavior of people in disasters   155.935
13. Electricity from the wind   621.312 136
14. Cleaning clothes at home   648.1
15. Sculpture in wax and wood   731.2

EXERCISE 6.5

1.   Ethiopia under Italian rule   963.057
2.   Drawing and preparing maps   526
3.   Social responsibility of executive management   658.408
4.   Talismans in witchcraft   133.44
5.   Rules of Parliament   060.42

6.	Detergent technology		668.14
7.	Military intelligence		355.343 2
8.	Ultrasonic vibrations	(physics)	534.55
		or (engineering)	620.28
9.	Design of roadworks	(engineering)	625.725
		or (area planning)	711.73
10.	Sculpture in the twentieth century		735.23
11.	Plant diseases		571.9
12.	Speed drills for typing		652.307
13.	The ethics of government		172.2
14.	Music for the guitar		787.87
15.	Discipline in the classroom		371.102 4
16.	Zodiac: an astrological guide		133.52
17.	Making trousers commercially		687.113
18.	Looking after your pet canary		636.686 25

EXERCISE 6.6

1.	A general introduction to the violin and other bowed string instruments	787.2
2.	Design and construction of clocks	681.113
3.	Cookery in restaurants	641.572
4.	How to code computer programs	005.13
5.	The use of radio in adult education	374.26
6.	Evolution of microbes	576.138
7.	Growing carrots in the home garden	635.13
8.	Techniques for indoor photography	778.72
9.	Eighteenth-century sculpture	735.21
10.	Manufacture of paper	676
11.	Triplets, quads and more: an obstetric guide	618.25
12.	The Panama Canal: modern aid to transportation	386.44
13.	The physics of auroras	538.768
14.	Flying fishes and seahorses: odd marine creatures	597.6
15.	A guide to cooking with pressure cookers	641.587

EXERCISE 7.1

1.	Dictionary of child psychology	155.403
2.	Journal of manufacture of electronic toys	688.728 05
3.	The language of soccer	796.334 014
4.	Pony weekly	636.160 5
5.	Teaching netball	796.324 071
6.	The philosophy of idealism	141
7.	The philosophy of social work	361.301
8.	Standards for lathes	621.942 021 8
9.	Dictionary of biochemistry	572.03
10.	A history of child care	649.109
11.	Systems of long-range weather forecasting	551.636 501 1
12.	Sales catalog of kitchen goods	643.302 94
13.	Guidebook for a toy museum	745.592 074
14.	The terrier encyclopedia	636.755 03
15.	Genetics research	576.507 2
16.	Handicrafts for people with disabilities	745.508 7

EXERCISE 7.2

The titles given are examples. Other titles covering the same topics are equally correct.

1.	796.352 05	Golf monthly
2.	370.3	The education encyclopedia
3.	371.003	A dictionary of school and special education
4.	372.03	A dictionary of elementary education
5.	375.000 3	A dictionary of curricula
6.	629.132 300 5	Aerodynamics quarterly
7.	181.005	The journal of Oriental philosophy
8.	336.002 85	Data processing in public finance
9.	621.388 007 2	Television research and development
10.	730.74	Sculpture museums
11.	300.724	Experimental research in the social sciences
12.	512.005	The journal of algebra and number theory
13.	512.705	The journal of number theory
14.	338.430 007 2	Industry investment research

EXERCISE 7.3

1.	Dictionary of library and information science	020.3
2.	Philosophy of library science	020.1
3.	Library and information science: a journal	020.5
4.	Dictionary of psychology	150.3
5.	Psychology: historical research	150.722
6.	Dictionary of ethics	170.3
7.	Ethics: a quarterly journal	170.5
8.	Epidemiology: psychological principles	614.401 9
9.	Dictionary of architecture	720.3
10.	Study and teaching of chemical technology	660.07

EXERCISE 7.4

1.	Popular engineering (quarterly journal)		620.005
2.	Agricultural pest control index		632.905
3.	Techniques and apparatus used in puppetry		791.530 28
4.	Correspondence courses in electronics		621.381 071 5
5.	Cookery in the Middle Ages		641.509 02
6.	Encyclopedia of horses		599.665 503
		or	636.100 3
7.	History of the social sciences		300.9
8.	Philosophy of Christianity		230.01
9.	Historical research into public administration		351.072 2
10.	Lives of ten great artists		700.922
11.	Theory of the solar system		523.201
12.	Research in oceanography		551.460 072
13.	Trotting monthly		798.460 5
14.	Theory of personnel management		658.300 1
15.	Book publishing trade catalogs		070.502 94
16.	Journal of the philosophy of socialism		335.001

REVIEW QUIZ 7.5

1. Standard subdivisions enable the classifier to make the number more specific by representing a regularly recurring form or treatment as well as the main subject.

2. They can almost always be added freely, when needed, to any classification number, although only one is added for any one work.

3. The number is shown as T1-.

4.   • When the number is already built into the schedules.
     • When they would be redundant because the number already covers the concept of the standard subdivision.
     • When there is an instruction not to use the standard subdivisions.
     • When the subject of the work is more specific than the classification number.

5.   -01 Philosophy and theory
     -03 Dictionaries, encyclopedias, concordances
     -05 Serial publications
     -07 Education, research, related topics
     -09 Historical, geographic, persons treatment.

6. To ensure that these "standard" treatments of the subject can be shelved in their groups before the subject is further subdivided.

7. There are many numbers which have a nonstandard procedure for the use of standard subdivisions.

8. 545.009.

9. The table at the beginning of Table 1, which indicates which standard subdivision to use if there is more than one possible standard subdivision representing different aspects of the topic.

10. -028, which comes before -07 in the table of preference.

EXERCISE 8.1

1.	The geography of Zimbabwe	916.891
2.	A textbook of the geography of Alaska	917.98
3.	The Amazon River: a geography	918.11
4.	Geography of ancient Rhodes	913.916
5.	A guidebook for travel in the French Riviera	914.490 4
6.	The travelers' guide to Spain	914.604
7.	Prehistoric geography of Carthage	913.973 01
8.	An illustrated guide to the geography of ancient England	913.620 022 2
		or 913.620 4
9.	A gazetteer of Southern Africa	916.800 3
10.	Bahrain: travel in the twentieth century	915.365 04

EXERCISE 8.2

1.	A history of ancient Sparta	938.9
2.	A short history of the mountain regions of Bolivia	984.1

3.	The causes of World War II	940.531 1
4.	The United States under Ronald Reagan	973.927
5.	A history of the Thirty Years War	940.24
6.	The French Revolution	944.04
7.	The Russian Revolution	947.084 1
8.	History of the Persian Empire	935.05
9.	Norway in the 1950s: an outline history	948.104 5
10.	The encyclopedia of Zambian history	968.940 03

EXERCISE 8.3

1.	Geology of Quebec	557.14
2.	Printmaking in Japan	769.952
3.	General statistics of Hungary	314.39
4.	Political conditions in the Irish Republic	320.941 7
5.	Economic conditions in Algeria	330.965
6.	Higher education in Vietnam	378.597
7.	Libraries in New Zealand	027.093
8.	The Roman Catholic Church in Paraguay	282.892
9.	Constitutional law of ancient China	342.31
10.	Life expectancy in Burundi	304.645 675 72

EXERCISE 8.4

1.	Snowmobiling in Scotland	796.940 941 1
2.	New Orleans brass bands	784.909 763 35
3.	Design and construction of buildings in Nagasaki	721.095 224 4
4.	Working mothers in ancient Rome	331.440 937 6
5.	Family counseling in Sweden	362.828 609 485

EXERCISE 8.5

The titles given are examples. Other titles covering the same topics are equally correct.

1.	942.052 007 2	Historical research on England in the reign of Henry VIII
2.	954.035 005	Journal of twentieth-century Indian history
3.	306.743 094 93	Male prostitution in Belgium
4.	283.753	The Episcopal Diocese of Washington, D.C.
5.	372.959 3	Elementary education in Thailand
6.	996.11	A short history of Fiji
7.	359.009 611	The Tunisian navy
8.	759.949 2	Painting and paintings of the Netherlands
9.	026.340 257 663 8	A directory of law librarians / libraries in Oklahoma City
10.	974.710 430 92	Famous New Yorkers of the twentieth century (1945-1999)

EXERCISE 8.6

1.	Raising pigs	636.4
2.	How to make soft toys	745.592 4
3.	Surfacing dirt roads	625.75
4.	Mobility of labor	331.127
5.	Food and shelter for the needy	361.05

6.	The encyclopedia of household pets	636.088 703
7.	Teaching drawing	741.07
8.	The theory of underwater photography	778.730 1
9.	The philosophy of evolution	576.801
		or 116
10.	Correspondence course in mathematics	510.715
11.	Radio in the 1930s	384.540 904 3
12.	The sociology of slavery in the Roman Empire	306.362 093 7
13.	Death customs in ancient Britain	393.093 61
14.	Theater in Zimbabwe	792.096 891
15.	Air pollution controls in Mexico	628.530 972
16.	Political parties in Peru	324.285
17.	Alligators of the Everglades	597.980 975 939
18.	Gold mining in Nevada	622.342 209 793
19.	Firefighting in Quebec Province	628.925 097 14
20.	Firefighting in the Gatineau Park (Quebec)	628.925 097 142 21

EXERCISE 8.7

1.	Modern archeology: techniques and equipment	930.102 8
2.	The dictionary of place names	910.3
3.	Maps of Irian Jaya	912.951
4.	Connecticut during the Colonial period	974.602
5.	Scotland in the 1960s	941.108 56
6.	Ohio history quarterly	977.100 5
7.	The diplomatic history of World War II	940.532
8.	Exploration of the moon	919.910 4
9.	Lake fishing	799.109 169 2
10.	Marine transportation across the Atlantic Ocean	387.509 163
11.	Baboons of the grasslands	599.865 091 53
12.	Wind systems in valleys	551.518 091 44
13.	Paintings in the seventeenth century	759.046
14.	Ancient Egypt during the Middle Kingdom	932.013
15.	The Thai Historical Association journal	959.300 5
16.	Life expectancy in Spain	304.645 46
17.	Modern British philosophy	192
18.	Customs of Easter Island	390.099 618
19.	Dictionary of building	690.03
20.	Experimental research in pharmaceutical chemistry	615.190 072 4

EXERCISE 9.1

1.	American (in English)	81
2.	Dutch	839.31
3.	Swedish	839.7
4.	French	84
5.	Italian	85
6.	Catalan	849.9
7.	Portuguese	869
8.	Classical Greek	88
9.	Urdu	891.439
10.	Assamese	891.451

11.	Breton	891.68
12.	Slovak	891.87
13.	Kota	894.81
	(Note that this is not a base number)	
14.	Korean	895.7
15.	Xhosa	896.398 5

EXERCISE 9.2

1.	Poetry by an American poet	811
2.	A drama in Dutch by one author	839.312
3.	A collection of a Swedish novelist	839.73
4.	Short stories in English translation by a French author	843
5.	Letters written by a high-ranking Italian lady	856
6.	Speeches in Catalan by a famous politician	849.95
7.	A Portuguese author's miscellaneous writings	869.8
8.	Classical Greek poetry by a medieval poet	881.02
9.	Twentieth-century drama by an Urdu author	891.439 27
10.	A modern Assamese novel	891.451 37
11.	Letters by a sixteenth-century Breton	891.686 1
12.	Speeches by a Slovenian citizen in 1920-1930	891.845 5
13.	Poems of a Kota woman	894.81
	(Do not add from Table 3—this is not a base number)	
14.	Reminiscences of a Korean during the Yi period	895.782 03
15.	Xhosa fiction	896.398 53

EXERCISE 9.3

1.	The Penguin book of Chinese verse	895.11
2.	Fifteenth-century English drama	822.2
3.	French essays between the wars	844.912
4.	A yearbook of Finnish literature	894.541 05
5.	Selected essays of Umberto Eco translated from the Italian (late twentieth century)	854.914
6.	War and peace, a novel by Leo Tolstoy, translated from the Russian	891.733
7.	Mother Courage and her children, by Berthold Brecht, a tragedy translated from German, written 1936-1939	832.912
8.	Letters home: letters of Sylvia Plath, U.S. poet, late twentieth century	816.54
9.	Famous Greek ballads of the nineteenth century	889.104 4
10.	The Spanish love story	863.085

EXERCISE 9.4

1.	A collection of poetry for children	821.008 092 82
	82 English language literature (schedules - base number)	
	1 + 00 poetry (Table 3B)	
	80 collections (Table 3B: from -1-8)	
	9282 for children (Table 3C)	

2. An anthology of American poetry about animals   811.008 036 2
     81   American literature in English (schedules - base number)
     1 + 00   poetry (Table 3B)
     80   collections (Table 3B: from -1-8)
     362   about animals (Table 3C)

3. Poems by English women, Elizabethan to Victorian   821.008 092 87
     82   English language literature (schedules - base number)
     1 + 00   poetry (Table 3B)
     80   collections (Table 3B: from -1-8)
     9287   by women (Table 3C)
Note: the period is not included, since it is too broad

4. An anthology of modern American plays   812.540 8
     81   American literature in English (schedules - base number)
     2   drama (Table 3B)
     54   1945-1999 (period table from schedules)
     08   collections (Table 3B: from -1-8)

5. The Faber book of contemporary Latin American short stories   863.010 886 8
     86   Spanish language literature (schedules - base number)
     301   short stories (Table 3B)
     08   collections (Table 3B: from -102-108)
     8   literature ... by persons of national groups (Table 3C)
     68   Spanish Americans (Table 5)

6. Best sellers by French teenagers   843.009 928 3
     84   French language literature (schedules - base number)
     3 + 00   fiction (Table 3B)
     9   history ... critical appraisal (Table 3B: from -1-8)
     9283   by teenagers (Table 3C)

7. A critical study of Manx literature   891.640 9
     891.64   Manx language literature (schedules - base number)
     09   history ... critical appraisal of works in more than one form (Table 3B)

8. Soviet literature of the 1980s: a decade of transition   891.709 004 4
     891.7   Russian language literature (schedules - base number)
     0900   history ... critical appraisal of works in more than one form (Table 3B) — literature from specific periods
     44   1945-1991 (period table from schedules)

9. The Virago book of ghost stories   823.087 33
     82   English language literature (schedules - base number)
     308733   ghost fiction (Table 3B)

10. The journal of Beatrix Potter from 1881-1897   828.803
     82   English language literature (schedules - base number)
     8   miscellaneous writings (Table 3A)
     8   1837-1899 (period table from schedules)
     03   diaries (Table 3A: from -81-89)

11. The grotesque in the arts   700.415
    700.4   Arts displaying specific qualities of style, mood, viewpoint (schedules—base
                   number)
        15   grotesque (Table 3C)

12. Comedy films   791.436 17
    791.436   Special aspects of films (schedules—base number)
        17   Comedy (Table 3C)

EXERCISE 10.1

1. Mind your spelling (how to spell English words)   correct
2. Let's learn our ABCs   correct
3. A Chinese reader   495.186
4. Street French: slang, idioms, and popular expletives (a historical approach)   correct
5. A crossword dictionary   423.1

EXERCISE 10.2

1. The Russian alphabet   491.711
2. The history of Hebrew   492.409
3. A new Lao reader   495.919 186
4. Spanish pronunciation   468.1
5. Modern German slang   437.09
6. A handbook of Malay script   499.281 1
7. Speak standard Indonesian   499.221 834
8. Teach yourself Swahili   496.392 824
9. English Creoles of the Caribbean   427.972 9
10. Portuguese as spoken in Brazil   469.798

EXERCISE 10.3

1. A quick beginners course in Hindi for English speakers   correct
2. Speak Greek in a week (for English-speaking persons)   489.383 421
3. Arabic phrase book (for English-speaking persons)   492.783 421
4. Fluent English for Danish speakers   428.343 981
5. A Dutch-English dictionary   439.313 21
6. A Japanese-German/German-Japanese dictionary   495.633 1

EXERCISE 10.4

1. A French-Vietnamese dictionary   443.959 22
2. A Khmer-English/English-Khmer dictionary   495.932 321
3. Spanish words in the English language   422.451
4. Serial publications in Tagalog   059.992 11
5. Folktales in Yiddish   398.204 391

EXERCISE 11.1

1.	Social anthropology of the Kurdish people	306.089 915 97
2.	Social anthropology of French-Canadians	306.089 114
3.	Bedouin art	704.039 272
4.	Afrikaner folk music	781.623 936
5.	Social services to Catalans	362.844 9
6.	Metal engraving of Portuguese-speaking people	765.089 69
7.	Child-rearing practices of the ancient Romans	649.108 971
8.	Polynesian football players	796.330 899 94
9.	Rum distilled by South American native people	641.259 089 98
10.	Palestinian Christians	270.089 927 4

EXERCISE 11.2

1.	Chemistry for potters	540.247 38
2.	The ethics of psychologists	174.915
3.	Preschool children as artists	704.054 3
4.	The art of North American native peoples	704.039 7
5.	Aerodynamics for ornithologists	533.620 245 98
6.	Choreography for opera singers	792.820 247 82
7.	An anthology of poetry by well-known detectives	821.008 092 363 2
8.	Lesbian TV stars	791.450 866 43
9.	Eritrean cooking in Los Angeles	641.592 928 097 949 4
10.	Civil and political rights in Muslim countries	323.091 767 1

EXERCISE 12.1

The titles given are examples. Other titles covering the same topics are equally correct.

1.	940.316 2	Pacifists in World War I
2.	025.171 6	Managing collections of rare library material
3.	255.530 09	A history of the Jesuit order
4.	725.210 87	Design of shopping centers for disabled people
5.	782.107 941	British opera festivals

EXERCISE 12.2

1.	Financial journalists and journalism	070.449 332
2.	Snakes in the Bible	220.859 796
3.	Commerce in the Koran	297.122 838 01
4.	Conversion of non-Jews to Judaism in India	296.714 095 4
5.	Diseases in corn crops	633.159 3
6.	Restoration of commercial buildings	725.202 88
7.	Care of games in libraries	025.179 6
8.	Learning about crocodiles from museums	597.980 75
9.	Scientific works as literature	809.935 5
10.	Raising goats as stunt animals	636.391 8

EXERCISE 13.1

1.	A guide to coffee table design	749.3
2.	Growing begonias	635.933 627

3.	The law of income tax		343.052
4.	Aerial photography	(general)	778.35
		or (military)	623.72
5.	Upholstering your sofa	(household)	645.4
		or (design)	747.5

EXERCISE 13.2
1.	The Crusades	correct
2.	Radio advertising	659.142
3.	The Apostles' Creed	correct

EXERCISE 13.3
1.	Causes of unemployment	331.137 2
2.	Schools of linguistics	410.18
3.	Modern British sheep breeds	636.32
4.	Modern art	709.04
5.	Church architecture	726.5

EXERCISE 13.4
1.	Chemical contraception		613.943 2
2.	Educating children with communicative disorders		371.914
3.	Sports injuries		617.102 7
4.	Fashion modeling		746.92
		or (advertising)	659.152
5.	Bringing up children		649.1

EXERCISE 13.5
1.	496.398 5	Xhosa language
2.	551.642 53	Frost—cold spell—weather-forecasting
3.	077.31	Journalism in Moscow

EXERCISE 13.6
1.	Etruscan sculpture	733.4
2.	Dinosaurs	567.9
3.	Halley's comet	523.642
4.	A history of drug addiction	362.290 9
5.	Having twins: a parent's guide to pregnancy, birth and early childhood	618.25

EXERCISE 14.1
1.	005.373 5	Specific computer programs
2.	070.593	Private publishers
3.	133.54	Horoscopes
4.	155.937	Death and dying
5.	268.67	Dramatic method in religious education

6.	303.484	Social innovation and change
7.	920.72	Biographies of women
8.	590.734 6	Zoos of Spain
9.	428.42	Remedial reading
10.	423.1	Dictionary of acronyms and abbreviations
11.	509.2	Scientists
12.	428.405	A journal about reading
13.	658.45	Communication in management
14.	786.509 2	Organists
15.	796.358 082	Women basketballers

EXERCISE 14.2

1.	Thailand: description and travel	915.930 4
2.	Wisconsin: discovery and exploration (1795-1869)	917.750 43
3.	Vancouver Island (B.C.): description and travel in the nineteenth century	917.112 042
4.	Asia: description and travel in the 1980s	915.044 28
5.	The waterfalls of Hawaii: a description	919.690 969 4
6.	Natural monuments in Central America: a pictorial work	719.320 972 8
7.	The Rand McNally guide to the coasts of Massachusetts, New Hampshire and Maine (a work designed to show points of interest in the 1980s)	917.404 43
8.	A guidebook for travel in Colorado	917.880 4
9.	An illustrated guide to the geography of ancient England	913.620 022 2
10.	Geographic features of ancient Rhodes	913.916
11.	Travel in India during 318-500 A.D.	913.404 6
12.	The cities of ancient Egypt: a geography	913.209 173 2
13.	Prehistoric geography of Carthage	913.973 01
14.	Maps of Yellowstone National Park	912.787 52
15.	Atlas of the ancient world	912.3

EXERCISE 14.3

1.	Atlas of the oceans of the world	912.196 2
2.	Physical geography of mountains	910.021 43
3.	An illustrated atlas of islands	912.194 200 222
4.	Maps of the Mediterranean Sea in the eighteenth century	912.196 380 903 3
5.	Maps of the ancient Roman Empire	912.37
6.	Spiritualism in Catholic countries	133.909 176 12
7.	Trade unions in Argentina	331.880 982
8.	Social welfare services to the mentally ill in British Columbia	362.209 711
9.	A guide to the snakes of Ireland	597.960 941 5
10.	Rail passenger transport in Belgium	385.220 949 3
11.	Printmaking in France	769.944
12.	Waterbirds of the world	598.176
13.	Local government in the Southern Hemisphere	320.809 181 4
14.	Birds of the Indian Ocean	598.091 65
15.	A guide to wine making in Virginia	663.200 975 5

EXERCISE 14.4

1.	Transplants in Transylvania	617.950 949 84
2.	The paintings of Tom Thomson	759.11
3.	Postage stamps of Angola	769.569 673
4.	Country music from Texas	781.642 097 64
5.	Horse racing tracks in Hong Kong	798.400 685 125
6.	Horse riding in Wyoming	798.230 978 7
7.	Hunting in South Africa in the nineteenth century	799.296 809 034
8.	German Christian church architecture of the sixteenth century	726.509 43
9.	*The Sydney Morning Herald* & other Sydney newspapers	079.944 1
10.	Folksongs of Chile	781.620 098 3
11.	Dutch narrative poetry	839.311 03
12.	Spanish farce	862.052 32
13.	Twentieth-century Spanish drama	862.6
14.	The modern Indonesian novel—the works of Pramoedya Ananta Toer	899.221 32
15.	An Indonesian dictionary	499.221 3

EXERCISE 14.5

1.	English-Indonesian dictionary	423.992 21
2.	English-Indonesian-English dictionary	499.221 321
3.	Dictionary of Indonesian acronyms	499.221 31
4.	Use of French words in English	422.441
5.	English for Spanish people	428.346 1
6.	English for Malayalam-speaking people	428.349 481 2
7.	Choral singing for the hearing impaired	782.508 72
8.	Case histories in psychiatry	616.890 9
9.	Pasteur the chemist: a biography	540.92
10.	General biology: a quarterly magazine	570.5
11.	A guide to fascist political theory	320.533
12.	Harrap's Russian dictionary	491.73
13.	The Roman Catholic Church in Spain	282.46
14.	The journal of sports medicine	617.102 705
15.	Kenya before the British	967.620 1

EXERCISE 14.6

1.	How to read maps	912.014
2.	Make-up for pantomime	792.302 7
3.	The ethics of euthanasia	179.7
4.	Biographies of ancient Egyptians	920.032
5.	Biographies of notable Jamaicans	920.072 92
6.	The movement for women's suffrage	324.623
7.	The Pankhursts: a biography	324.623 092 2
8.	Modern archeology: techniques and equipment	930.102 8
9.	Genealogical sources of Scotland	929.341 1
10.	An introduction to historiography	907.2
11.	The spiritual discipline of yoga	291.436
12.	Erotica in art	700.453 8
13.	Design of caravan parks for long-term residents	711.58
14.	An introduction to mechanical pumps	621.6
15.	Dictionary of biology	570.3

Exercise 14.7

1.	Dutch poetry of the seventeenth century	839.311 3
2.	The design of motels for the aged	728.508 46
3.	First aid for gunshot wounds	617.145 026 2
4.	Scotland under James II	941.104
5.	Modern joinery: a guide to North American practice	694.609 7
6.	Preparing microscopic plant slides	580.282 7
7.	Scale models of solar-powered automotive engines	629.221 95
8.	Manufacture of toilet tissue: patents	676.284 202 72
9.	Research in the manufacture of hand tools	621.908 072
10.	Underwriting health and accident insurance	368.380 12
11.	English fiction: a secondary school study guide	823.007 12
12.	The Robben Island prison riot	365.641 096 873 5
13.	The San Diego Museum of Art	708.194 98 (city) or 708.194 985 (county)
14.	The design of tugboats	623.812 32
15.	A zoological study of clams, mussels & cuttlefish	594

Exercise 14.8

1.	549.911	Minerals of the polar regions
2.	513.071 2	Teaching arithmetic in secondary schools
3.	634.709 777	Growing berries in Iowa
4.	853.914	Italian fiction since 1945
5.	912.431 55	Berlin street directory
6.	978.112 5	The history of Rawlins County
7.	025.065 786 809 759	Information storage and retrieval systems devoted to endangered species in Florida
8.	004.015 1	Mathematical principles of computer science
9.	285.295 95	The Presbyterian Church of Vanuatu
10.	296.830 974 811	The history of the Jewish community in Philadelphia
11.	305.488 950 73	Burmese women in the United States
12.	324.630 899 755	Elections for Iroquois Indians
13.	338.274 309 959 2	Copper mining in Bougainville
14.	362.102 308 2	Women carers of people with physical illnesses
15.	378.33	International fellowships in higher education

Exercise 14.9

1.	Traditional Jewish rites: Bar mitzvah	296.442 4
2.	Research into the manufacture of synthetic perfumes	668.544 072
3.	Collecting pistols	623.443 207 5
4.	The Kansas City Jazz Festival	781.653 079 781 39
5.	How to lip-read	371.912 7
6.	Corals of the Australian Barrier Reef	593.609 943
7.	Canada under Trudeau	971.064 4
8.	The building of rock-fill dams in the nineteenth century	627.830 903 4
9.	Nursing aged psychiatric patients	610.736 5
10.	Nebraska between the World Wars	978.203 2
11.	Residential care for heroin addicts	362.293 85
12.	Prostitution in the twentieth century: a sociological study	306.740 904
13.	Photographs of animals	779.32

| 14. | Rotary clubs in South Carolina | 369.520 975 7 |
| 15. | The mining of tin | 622.345 3 |

EXERCISE 14.10

The titles given are examples. Other titles covering the same topics are equally correct.

1.	181.07	Islamic philosophy
2.	153.947 96	Tests for sporting ability
3.	155.911 67	Psychology of taste
4.	428.340 706 69	Education and research in English as a second language in Nigeria
5.	331.124 100 5	Job opportunities in science
6.	331.137 810 274	Unemployment for public library staff
7.	331.119 66	Labor force in chemical engineering
8.	331.252 916 59	Pensions in advertising and public relations
9.	331.413 7	Female unemployment
10.	338.372 757	Trout as a product
11.	336.266 73	Import taxes on sculpture
12.	230.98	Shakers' doctrines
13.	220.520 33	Concordance of the Bible (King James version)
14.	230.071 185	Higher education in Christian theology in Peru
15.	220.872 582 702 89	Safety measures for amphitheaters in the Bible

GLOSSARY

add To add in DDC means to attach or append a number to the end of another number—e.g., 636.825 + 39 = 636.82539

add note A note instructing the classifier to append (add) one number to another number

author number *See* book number

auxiliary table A table of numbers and/or letters which can be added to notation in the schedules to make a classification number more specific

base number The number found in the schedules of Dewey Decimal Classification to which a number can be added from the tables

Bibliographic Classification (BC) A classification scheme devised by H. E. Bliss, using letters and numbers. Completely revised in 1976, but not widely used

Bliss Classification *See* Bibliographic Classification

book number The numbers, letters, or combination of numbers and letters used to distinguish an individual item from other items with the same classification number

broad classification Classification using the main divisions and subdivisions of a scheme without breaking down into narrower concepts

built number A number not printed in the schedules which is built by beginning with a base number and adding another number to it

call number A number on a library item consisting of a classification number, a book number and often a location symbol

caption *See* heading

CC *See* Colon Classification

centered heading A heading in Dewey Decimal Classification which applies to a range of classification numbers

citation order The order in which two or more aspects of a topic are combined in number building

class The broadest grouping of numbers in a classification scheme representing a subject group or discipline—e.g., religion

class-elsewhere note A note giving the classifier the location of related topics

classification A system for arranging library materials according to subject

classification number Number allocated to a library item to indicate a subject

classification scheme A particular scheme for arranging library materials according to subject—e.g., Dewey Decimal Classification, Library of Congress Classification

classified catalog A catalog in which the entries are arranged in order of classification number

classify To allocate a classification number

close classification Classifying as specifically as possible, using all available subdivisions of a scheme

collocation Arrangement which locates like material together

Colon Classification (CC) A classification scheme devised by S. R. Ranganathan for Indian libraries, using numbers and letters and a colon to separate different parts of the classification number

complete revision A revision in which virtually all the subdivisions of a part of the schedule are changed; formery called a phoenix schedule

comprehensive number A number which covers all the aspects of the subject within a discipline

co-ordinate A number or topic at the same level as another number or topic in the same hierarchy

Cutter number A system of author numbers, devised by Charles A. Cutter, beginning with the first letter of the author's name and followed by numbers. Used in Library of Congress Classification for authors, titles and geographic areas

Cutter-Sanborn number An extension of the Cutter author number system, outlined in the Cutter-Sanborn Three-Figure Author Table. Designed to maintain works with the same classification number in alphabetical order of author

DDC *See* Dewey Decimal Classification

definition note A note giving the meaning of a term in a heading

Dewey Decimal Classification DDC. A classification scheme, devised by Melvil Dewey in 1873, using numbers to represent subjects

discipline A very broad group of subjects in a classification scheme—e.g., social science

discontinued number A number from a previous edition which is no longer used. These numbers are shown in square brackets—e.g., [361.323]

division The second level of subdivision in Dewey Decimal Classification, represented by the first two digits of the notation—e.g., 51 in 510 (Mathematics)

enumerative classification Classification which attempts to spell out (enumerate) all the single and composite subjects required—e.g., Library of Congress Classification

EPC Dewey Decimal Classification Editorial Policy Committee. An international committee of experts which advises on the development of the Dewey Decimal Classification scheme

extensive revision A major reworking of some subdivisions without altering the main outline of the schedule

facet An aspect or orientation of a topic

facet indicator A digit used to introduce notation representing an aspect, or facet, of a subject—e.g., the 0 in standard subdivisions like -09

faceted classification Classification which allows for notation to be built up by the use of tables and other parts of the schedules. All modern classification schemes are faceted to a degree. Colon Classification is the definitive faceted classification scheme

first summary The ten classes, each of which represents a broad discipline or group of disciplines

first-of-two rule The rule which requires a work covering two subjects in the same discipline to be classified at the number coming first in the schedules

fixed location Items are labeled according to their physical location, rather than their intellectual content

form 1. The way in which bibliographic text is arranged—e.g., dictionary. 2. Type of literary work—e.g., poetry, drama

form class Used for literature. Items are classified not according to subject, but according to their literary form—e.g., poetry, drama

form division Used for works on any subject which are presented in a particular bibliographic form—e.g., dictionary, periodical

generalia class Used for very general topics and comprehensive combinations of topics—e.g., current affairs, general encyclopedias

heading A name, word or phrase used to name a classification number

hierarchical classification Classification in which the division of subjects is from the most general to the most specific—e.g., Dewey Decimal Classification

hierarchical force The principle that each topic in a class is subordinate to and part of all the broader topics above it

hierarchy The ranked order of subjects in a classification scheme

including note A note enumerating topics which are included in the number but are less extensive than the heading. Standard subdivisions may not be added to the numbers for these topics

index 1. An alphabetical list of terms or topics in a work, usually found at the back. 2. A systematically arranged list which indicates the contents of a document or group of documents

integrated shelving Shelving in which all physical formats of material are shelved in one sequence

interdisciplinary number A number covering a subject from the perspective of more than one discipline, including the discipline where the number is located

Library of Congress Classification A classification scheme developed by the Library of Congress, using numbers and letters

literary warrant The volume of books written, or likely to be written, on a topic

location Where an item is housed. This can be the name of the library or the part of a collection

location symbol A symbol showing which collection an item belongs to—e.g., "F" for fiction

mixed notation A combination of types of symbol—e.g., numbers and letters used in Library of Congress Classification

mnemonic Aiding memory

Moys Classification A specialized classification scheme for law, devised by Edith Moys, based on the law schedule of Library of Congress Classification

notation The series of symbols which stand for the classes, subclasses, divisions and subdivisions of classes

notational synthesis *See* number building

number building Construction of classification numbers not listed in the schedules, following rules given in the scheme for combining numbers

option An alternative to the standard notation, provided to give emphasis to a particular aspect of a library's collection

pattern entry One or more numbers in the schedules using standard subdivisions in a particular pattern

phoenix schedule *See* complete revision

preference order The order indicating which one number is chosen when there is more than one possible number representing different aspects of the topic

pure notation One type of symbol only—e.g., numbers—used as the notation of a classification scheme

reduction Making a classification number shorter by omitting one or more groups of digits from the end of the number

related term A subject heading at the same level of specificity to another heading and related in subject matter

relative index In a classification scheme, an alphabetical list of all topics and synonyms, showing the relation of the topics to all the disciplines with which they are associated

relative location Items are classified in relationship to others depending on the subject

relocated topic A subject which has been given a different classification number

relocation Moving a topic to a new number in a new edition

revision An alteration of the text of DDC. There are three degrees of revision: routine revision—updating terminology, clarifying notes, providing modest expansions; extensive revision—a major reworking of subdivisions, without altering the main outline of the schedule; complete revision—virtually all the subdivisions of a part of the schedule are changed

routine revision Updating terminology, clarifying notes, and providing modest expansions

rule of application The rule that a work about the application of one subject to a second subject is classified with the second subject

rule of three The rule that a work which gives equal treatment to three or more subjects that are all subdivisions of a broader subject is classified with the first higher number which includes all of them

rule of zero The rule that subdivisions beginning with 0 should be avoided if there is a choice between 0 and subdivisions beginning with 1-9. Similarly, avoid subdivisions beginning with 00 if there is a choice between 0 and 00

schedule The enumerated classes, divisions, etc., of a classification scheme, arranged in number order

scope note A note describing the range and meaning of a term or classification number, especially where the use of the number is broader or narrower than is apparent from the heading

second summary The 100 divisions, each of which represents a broad topic

see also reference A direction from one heading to another when both are used

see reference A direction from one heading which is not used to another heading which is used

segmentation The division of classification numbers into meaningful parts, with a view to abbreviating them for a particular library

shelf list The record of the works in a library in the order in which they are shelved

specific index An alphabetical list which gives one entry only for each topic mentioned in the schedules, together with synonyms

standard subdivision An auxiliary number in Dewey Decimal Classification which represents a standard form or treatment of a subject—e.g., -09 for historical treatment

standing room Where a topic does not have enough literature to have its own number. The topic is narrower than the number in which it is included, and number building is not allowed. This leaves open the possibility of adding a more specific number to a future edition

subdivision A section of a classification scheme or subject heading

subordinate At a lower or more specific level than another number or topic in the same hierarchy

summary A listing of the main classes, divisions, sections or subdivisions, which provides an overview of the structure

superordinate At a higher or broader level than another number or topic in the same hierarchy

synthesis The process of constructing a number by adding notation from the tables or other parts of the schedules to a base number

synthetic classification Classification which allows the classifier to construct (synthesize) numbers for composite subjects—e.g., Colon Classification, Universal Decimal Classification

table A set of numbers in a classification scheme which are added to a number from the schedules to make a more specific number

table of preference A list of numbers indicating the order (preference order) in which they are to be chosen if all aspects cannot be included

third summary The 1,000 sections, each of which is a whole number and represents a specific topic

UDC *See* Universal Decimal Classification

unique call number A number on a library item—consisting of a classification number, a book number and often a location symbol—which is different from every other call number in the library

Universal Decimal Classification (UDC) A classification scheme developed by the International Federation for Information and Documentation (FID) by expanding Dewey Decimal Classification. It offers the most specific classification for specialized collections and is widely used in special libraries

work mark A letter used in Cutter-Sanborn numbers to distinguish different titles by the same author

BIBLIOGRAPHY

Chan, Lois Mai, et al. *Dewey Decimal Classification: A Practical Guide,* 2nd ed. Albany, N.Y.: Forest Press, 1996.

Cutter, Charles Ammi. *Cutter-Sanborn Three-Figure Author Table,* Swanson-Swift revision. Littleton, Colo.: distributed by Libraries Unlimited, 1969.

Dewey, Melvil. *Dewey Decimal Classification and Relative Index,* 21st ed., edited by Joan S. Mitchell, Julianne Beall, Winton Matthews, Jr., and Gregory R. New, 4 vols. Albany, N.Y.: OCLC Forest Press, 1996.

Dewey for Windows. Dublin, Ohio: OCLC Forest Press, 1996.

Mitchell, Joan S. "DDC21 and Beyond: The Dewey Decimal Classification Prepares for the Future", *Cataloging and Classification Quarterly* 21(2): 37-47.

Wiegand, Wayne A. *Irrepressible Reformer: A Biography of Melvil Dewey.* Chicago: American Library Association, 1996.

Wynar, Bohdan S. *Introduction to Cataloging and Classification,* 8th ed. Englewood, Colo.: Libraries Unlimited, 1992.

INDEX

ABOUT THE AUTHOR

Mary Mortimer is a teacher, librarian, author, and publisher. She is a director of DocMatrix Pty Limited, and was coordinator of the Library Studies program at the Canberra Institute of Technology in Canberra, Australia. She is the coauthor of *CatSkill* (InfoTrain, 1998) and *US MARC Made Easy* (InfoTrain, 1997), which are interactive multimedia training programs for libraries, author of *Learn Descriptive Cataloging* and *LibrarySpeak* (Scarecrow, 2000), and contributor to many other publications.